O9-AHT-574

Canada's House

Canada's House
Rideau Hall
and the invention of a Canadian home

Margaret MacMillan
Marjorie Harris
and Anne L. Desjardins
in conversation with
Adrienne Clarkson and
John Ralston Saul

Principal house, garden, and food photography by
Nancy Tong, Tony Beck,
and Rob Fiocca

Alfred A. Knopf Canada with Otherwise Editions

PUBLISHED BY ALFRED A. KNOPF CANADA

Design Direction: Dinnick & Howells with Sara Angel

NATIONAL LIBRARY OF CANADA CATALOGUING IN PUBLICATION

MacMillan, Margaret Olwen
Canada's house : Rideau Hall and the invention of a Canadian home / Margaret MacMillan, Marjorie Harris, Anne L. Desjardins ; with Adrienne Clarkson and John Ralston Saul.

ISBN 0-676-97675-1

1. Rideau Hall (Ottawa, Ont.). 2. Gardens—Ontario—Ottawa. 3. Cookery, Canadian. I. Harris, Marjorie. II. Desjardins, Anne L. III. Title.

FC3096.8.R5M32 2004 971.3'84 C2004-901905-8

FIRST EDITION

www.randomhouse.ca

Printed and bound in Canada

10 9 8 7 6 5 4 3 2 1

p. ii: In a family photo from 1940 that sits on one of the bookshelves in Adrienne Clarkson's study, her parents, William and Ethel Poy, pose with her and her older brother, Neville.

p. iii: Lord Minto's daughters (*left to right*): Violet, Eileen, and Ruby.

p. iv: A detail of the portrait of Lord Tweedsmuir (John Buchan) that hangs in the Tent Room.

p. v: A detail of a Limoges plate commissioned by Pauline Vanier in 1967 to commemorate Canada's centennial (the crown is the emblem of Queen Elizabeth II).

p. vi: A view of the Long Gallery in 1945.

p. vii: Decorative pewter bowls by Raymond Cox of St. John's, Newfoundland and Labrador, sitting on an early nineteenth-century birch and cherry Nova Scotia table in the Large Drawing Room. In the background is an Upper Canadian moiré maple and birch chaise longue from the 1830s.

p. viii: View of Rideau Hall, circa 1878, from the Lower Terrace lawn.

p. ix: Virginia Bluebells *Mertensia pulmonarioides*, syn. *M. virginica* at the edge of Rideau Hall's grounds.

p. x (*facing title page*): Winter photo taken during the Lansdowne mandate.

p. xiii (*facing this page*): The Small Drawing Room at Rideau Hall has recently been repainted with colours true to its period. The artwork on the wall is *Sightline (Brilliant Orange)*, by Winnipeg artist Wanda Koop. This room brings together a trio of early nineteenth-century games tables by Thomas Nesbitt, the important furniture maker of Saint John, NB.

p. xiv (*facing contents page*): Past winners of the Governor General's Literary Awards line a shelf in the governor general's study.

p. xvii: The approach drive to Rideau Hall as seen from the front entrance, September 1918.

The Group of Seven in Western Canada

75c
THE PILLAR
David Walker
THE
NCREDIBLE
ANADIAN
HUTCHISO
LONGMANS
JOHN A.
MACDONALD
THE
YOUNG
POLITICIAN
DONALD
REIGHTON
Illustrated
MACMILLAN
reighton
JOHN A. MACDONALD
The Young Politician
acmillan
GREAT
MACMILLA

CONTENTS

The most ephemeral thing at Rideau Hall
is the governor general; all the rest is history.

MME GABRIELLE LÉGER

PART I

A Canadian House.

Rideau Hall is a piece of our picture of ourselves. It has grown to maturity along with the country. I like to think of the house as a physical manifestation of the office. Rideau Hall represents the continuity of the Canadian experience.

Conversations about the nature of Canada have been going on at Rideau Hall since before Confederation.

by Margaret MacMillan

CHAPTER I

An Emblem of Canada Rideau Hall has grown to maturity along with the country and has changed as Canada, and Canadians, have changed.

Front door, Rideau Hall, before 1882.

When you pass through the great ornamental gates that face 24 Sussex Drive, the residence of the prime minister, and follow the gentle slope of the drive through the park, you will be surprised by the large house you find. It is hidden from view until the last moment. Viceregal families and their guests have driven up this driveway since Charles Stanley Monck (Viscount Monck), governor general at the time of Confederation, laid it out when he moved here in 1865. You are following the route used by every important Canadian political figure since Confederation, from Sir John A. Macdonald to Paul Martin, and by foreign notables from Winston Churchill to Nelson Mandela and Vladimir Putin. Today some 150,000 visitors a year make the same journey to Rideau Hall. This is Canada's House, the home and workplace of the governor general, who, as representative of the Crown in Canada, acts as our head of state, our commander-in-chief, indeed as the figurehead of our democracy. Rideau Hall is a piece of our picture of ourselves. It has grown to maturity along with the country and has changed as Canada, and Canadians, have changed. It is an emblem of the Canada of today.

The early governors general were not always pleased with what they found. When young Hariot Blackwood (Countess of Dufferin) arrived in 1872 after a lengthy journey from Quebec City, she was dismayed to discover only "a long two-storied villa." To a friend in England she complained: "The house appears to me to be at the land's end, and there is no view whatever from it, though it is near the river—and we have come through hundreds of miles of splendid scenery to get to it!" Forty years later, the Duchess of Connaught had a similar reaction: "One wonders if one has made a mistake & come up to a gymnasium flanked by a riding school with a very poor little porch connecting the two?"

Rideau Hall was never meant to be the official residence of Canada's head of state. It was a gentleman's house, built by Thomas MacKay, a stonemason from Scotland who prospered as a contractor in the small lumber town known as Bytown and

Preceding pages: Detail of the Ballroom's silk curtains.

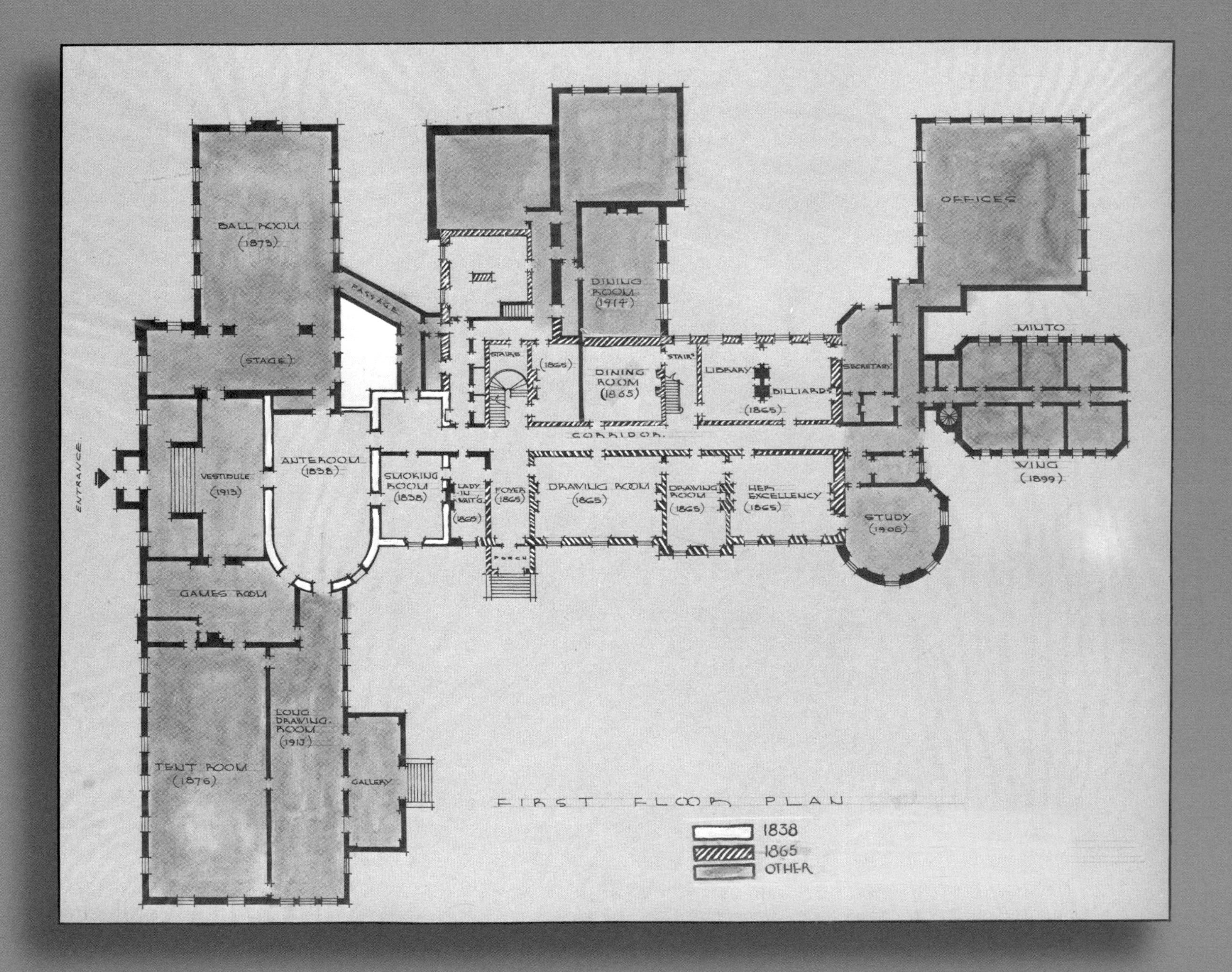

FIRST FLOOR PLAN
1838
1865
OTHER
ENTRANCE
BALL ROOM (1873)
(STAGE)
PASSAGE
VESTIBULE (1913)
ANTEROOM (1838)
GAMES ROOM
TENT ROOM (1876)
LONG DRAWING ROOM (1913)
GALLERY
SMOKING ROOM (1838)
LADY IN WAIT'G (1865)
FOYER (1865)
PORCH
STAIRS
(1865)
DINING ROOM (1865)
DINING ROOM (1914)
STAIRS
CORRIDOR
DRAWING ROOM (1865)
DRAWING ROOM (1865)
HER EXCELLENCY (1865)
LIBRARY
BILLIARDS (1865)
SECRETARY
STUDY (1906)
OFFICES
MINTO WING (1899)

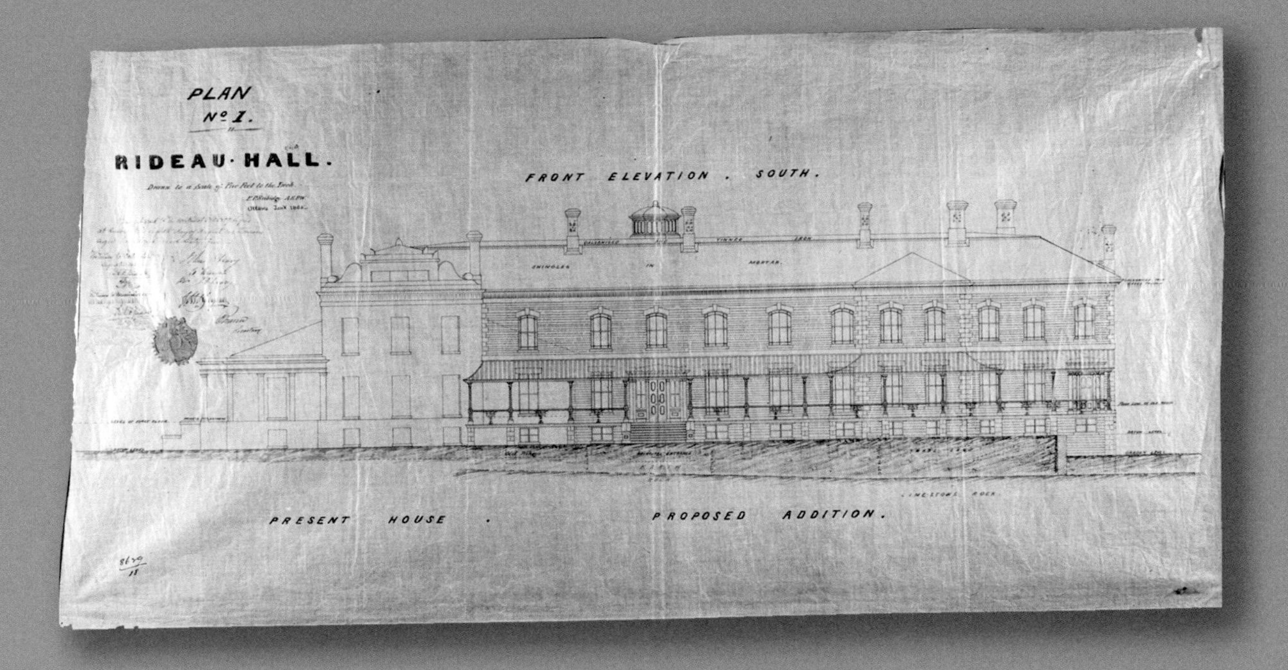

Opposite: A 1970s ground floor plan of Rideau Hall, indicating in white what remains of the original 1838 house and the dates of the various additions. The front entrance is at the bottom of the image. The area identified as the "Gallery" (with steps out into the garden) is now the glassed-in Verandah. *Above*: A plan of F.W. Rubidge's original addition to MacKay's 1838 villa, showing the south elevation facing what would become the ornamental gardens.

then went on to construct the Rideau Canal. With dreams of Georgian villas back in Britain, he built himself an elegant stone house with a classical bow front and two symmetrical wings.

In 1857, two years after MacKay's death, Ottawa, as Bytown had come to be known, was chosen as the capital of Canada (in those days the two provinces of Upper and Lower Canada). Work started on the Parliament Buildings, and elaborate plans were also drawn up for a suitable house for the governor general. But by 1864 there was still no Government House in Ottawa, so, as a temporary measure, the government leased Rideau Hall from the MacKay family. The Department of Public Works started redoing the house, adding a two-storey wing on the east side, leading off the back of the orig-

Below: Workers pose in front of Rideau Hall's new façade, completed in 1913 in what was described as "an adapted Florentine style." *Opposite*: A construction crew demolishing the west wing of Thomas MacKay's original villa in July 1913.

inal house. It was all a waste of money, George Brown, the leader of the opposition, told the first prime minister, Sir John A. Macdonald, who agreed.

All the same, in 1868 the government of the newly created confederation of Canada bought Rideau Hall outright—that "miserable little house," as Brown called it. None of its early occupants considered it adequate, but it became Canada's national house by default. When Frederick Blackwood (Earl of Dufferin) arrived as governor general in 1872, he added a ballroom and a tennis court, and three decades later Mary Elliot (Countess of Minto) extended the east wing to provide offices for staff and bedrooms for her family. All these changes were viewed as stop-gaps until a proper Government House could be built. Her husband, Gilbert Elliott (Earl of Minto), dreamed of handing Rideau Hall over for a National Gallery and building a grand residence for the governor general at Nepean Point, close to Parliament Hill with a proper view of the Ottawa River. When Albert Grey (Earl Grey) arrived in 1904, he preferred nearby Rockliffe Park's "surroundings of beauty, privacy and dignity, which would satisfy not only National but Imperial sentiment," but contented himself with more additions, building what is still the governor general's study and a new greenhouse. His successor, Prince Arthur, the Duke of Connaught, enlarged the dining room so it could hold eighty people (it has since been reduced in size and now seats 42), improved the servants' quarters, and, in 1913, added the front entrance we see today. The house has kept the same shape ever since.

When you arrive at Rideau Hall, you will be startled by this grand front, built in what was described at the time as "an adapted Florentine style." The massive pediment bears the royal coat of arms and, if you look at the peak, you will be able to tell if the governor general is in residence by the standard, with its gold lion on a blue field, that flies from the flag-pole. Go in under the great fanlight to the dignified Front Foyer with its marble staircase and an imposing ceiling studded with sunken panels and with portraits of the first two Canadian governors general, Vincent Massey and Georges Vanier, facing each other from either end. Climb the steps

and walk across the rose-coloured Tabriz carpet, through the arched doorway, and into the Reception Room, with its curved end. You are now in one of the few remaining parts of the original house, where Georgian symmetry had not yet given way to Victorian Gothic. Huge pieces of late Victorian ornamental silver share space with sculptures by contemporary Canadian artists, Tony Urquhart and Gathie Falk among others. From the walls, portraits of the Canadian governors general look out at you.

You may not realize it but you are standing at the hub of Rideau Hall. The house stretches out to either side and straight ahead. If you turn to your left (facing north) you will discover the great, blue Ballroom. Balls are rare today, but many formal dinners are held here for visiting heads of state, discussions among Canadians on the issues of the day, and public ceremonies such as investitures into the Order of Canada or the Bravery Awards. Apart from the House of Commons, this is the most photographed and televised room in Canada.

Turn to your right (facing south) from the Reception Room and you will find two long rooms. The larger of these, the Tent Room, was built in the 1870s as an indoor tennis court, though Lord Dufferin added canvas walls on occasion to make it another ballroom and some twenty years later, that great improver, Ishbel Gordon (Countess of Aberdeen), started this country's first portrait gallery here. The walls are now lined with every one of Canada's British governors general, from Lord Monck in the 1860s to Harold Alexander (Viscount Alexander of Tunis) in the 1950s. Rideau Hall has no ghosts, so they say, but the portrait of the sad and gentle John Campbell (Marquess of Lorne) always hangs crooked. The striped fabric on the walls nods to the Tent Room's past, but the floor is now marble, and no one has played tennis here since the 1960s.

If the great double doors are open, you can wander into the second room, the Long Gallery, which runs alongside the Tent Room. By one of the windows that overlook a formal garden, you will see Glenn Gould's Steinway, the one on which he practised at home. The carpets are blue-and-white Chinese; indeed, the Long Gallery has had a vaguely Chinese

Opposite: Jeanne Sauvé's striking portrait by Cleeve Horne grabs your attention as you move from the Front Foyer into the Reception Room. The neo-Gothic style oak chair was part of a set of furniture acquired by Rideau Hall in 1866. The papier mâché sculpture, entitled "*Dress with Candles*" (1998), is by Gathie Falk, on loan from the National Gallery of Canada.

Preceding pages: Despite having retained all its original Edwardian architectural features, including marble wainscotting and a coffered ceiling, Rideau Hall's Front Foyer is bright and airy. The console tables on either side of the entrance to the Reception Room were commissioned by the Canadiana Fund from Michael Fortune, one of Canada's foremost contemporary furniture designers. The commission was made possible through a donation by Mrs. Liliane M. Stewart. The woodwork includes unusual bigleaf maple with a blistered grain from British Columbia and cherry from central Canada; the table tops are Manitoulin Island limestone.

Above: The entrance area of the Ballroom with its proscenium-style arch (here as it looked during Lord Grey's tenure just before the First World War) doubled as a stage for amateur theatricals. *Opposite*: A glimpse of the Ballroom today as seen through an archway. AC: "In the early days of the British governors general, protocol was so strict that the viceregal couple could only dine and accept invitations from about a dozen people, such as the papal nuncio and the chief justice of Canada. In the last fifty years Canadian ways have prevailed. We can thank Norah Michener for putting an end to the practice of people curtseying."

Opposite: The Tent Room today. It was Gabrielle Léger in the 1970s who first turned the room into a portrait gallery of the British-born governors general. The Duke of Connaught is in the immediate foreground. Visible beyond him is the Earl of Minto. *Above left*: The original indoor tennis court, which was built in 1876 and inaugurated by Lord Dufferin. Over time it was increasingly used as a reception room or large dining room. *Above right*: For social events, the unsightly wooden walls and ceiling of the tennis court were covered with striped canvas, giving it the appearance of a large tent, which led to it being called the Tent Room. AC: "When you walk into the Tent Room you can still imagine those British governors general and their aides-de-camp bashing the ball about. These days we host a lot of important dinners and lunches there, because it seats around 170 people at seventeen or eighteen tables of eight or ten. The portraits make good conversation pieces. People will often ask about them. And the hosts at the tables, who are always members of the Rideau Hall staff, can identify them all."

A House and a Home

When you live at Rideau Hall, you walk every day through different periods of Canadian history, dating from before Confederation right up to the present. Like the country, the house has changed enormously over the years. There were times when it was very stiff and formal, in the worst sense of those words. It was a long time before the house and the gardens were truly opened up to Canadian citizens. Now it feels like a very friendly house, a place that has been lived in and loved. It's the kind of house where you'd like to be invited over, not only because the rooms are beautiful or the pictures on the walls are fine paintings by Canadian artists, but because, despite being on a large scale, it feels like a home.

Apart from the scale, the difference is that this home belongs to all Canadians, so we've tried to open it up even more than it has been in the past. Rideau Hall is now one of the ten most visited sites in Ottawa. We welcome people to tour the house and the gardens from May into October, every day, all day. The tours happen at regular times, you don't have to book them, and you don't have to pay. In fact, everything we offer to visitors is free: the house tours, the garden tours, the art tours, the summer concerts with Canadian performers from all over the country, the winter and summer parties. Canadians are invited to get acquainted with an essential part of their own history.

I like to think of the house as a physical manifestation of the office. And, as Gabrielle Léger so astutely observed, the governor general is here today, gone tomorrow. The house will be here a lot longer than we will. That's why it must be cherished and nurtured. Rideau Hall represents the continuity of the Canadian experience. *AC*

Glenn Gould's practice piano sits in the centre of the Long Gallery, where it is often played during Rideau Hall receptions. The red cedar screen in the background, created by the great Haida artist Bill Reid for Canada's centennial, is on loan from the Royal British Columbia Museum.

flavour ever since Lady Willingdon put a few pieces of lacquered furniture here in the 1920s. At one end stands a huge wooden screen carved from red cedar by the Haida artist Bill Reid. At the other hang two paintings by Emily Carr. From the Long Gallery you can walk out into the garden through the glassed-in Verandah, which was completely reconstructed by Roméo LeBlanc to make a room for informal breakfasts and lunches.

If you return to the hub of the Reception Room, and go straight ahead (east), you will pass through a small antechamber, its walls hung with paintings of the Second World War by such artists as Alex Colville and Lawren Harris, a reminder of the considerable part that war has played in our history. Beyond the antechamber lies the Monck Wing Corridor, which runs the length of the wing built in the 1860s and extended by Lady Minto and Lord Grey before the First World War to provide more office space. You pass a door festooned with apple blossoms, painted more than a century ago by Queen Victoria's daughter Princess Louise, when her husband, the Marquess of Lorne, was governor general. Ahead of you are dining rooms, one large, the other small (but only by comparison), reception rooms, and a library. Partway down, two stately staircases lead up to more hallways, bedrooms, private sitting rooms, and even a small chapel, created by the devout Vaniers. Visiting heads of state, the Queen or the president of

Above left: This photograph of Princess Louise's boudoir in what was known as the Blue Parlour (now the office of the governor general's spouse) shows one of the doors she painted with apple boughs. *Above right*: The Monck Wing Corridor (as it looked in 1945) is furnished with items that probably arrived with the Earl of Athlone and went back with him to England at the end of his mandate. *Opposite*: The only surviving painted door from Princess Louise's boudoir can now be seen from the Monck Wing Corridor. AC: "After Princess Louise lost part of her ear in a sleighing accident, she devoted herself more and more to her painting. And her husband decreed that she should spend no more winters in Canada. Maybe the apple boughs helped cheer her up."

This Door Was Painted By
H.R.H. Princess Louise
(Marchioness of Lorne)
in 1879

Above: The governor general's study as it looked in 1945, during the tenure of the Earl of Athlone. *Opposite:* The door opening from the Monck Wing Corridor into the governor general's study today. Paterson Ewen's *Sun Dogs #4*, on loan from the Art Gallery of Ontario, hangs on the right. The study's oval shape complements the rounded design of the original MacKay villa. AC: "I think my office has very good *feng shui*—*feng* is the Chinese for wind and *shui* means water—which is to say that it is well placed. It faces south and it gets the good winds. When I first moved in, the office had green broadloom that had been on the floor for about fifty years, threadbare in many places. When we lifted the broadloom we discovered this lovely oak floor underneath. It only needed to be sanded and polished."

South Africa, for example, always stay in the elegant Oval Suite. The whole interior is a pleasant surprise after the grandiloquence of the façade. This is no palace but a charmingly higgledy-piggledy sprawl that has grown this way and that over the years. It has, said Vincent Massey, "a certain lovable eccentricity. It is built in no particular style but rather in a progression of styles."

At the end of the corridor, to your right, past the study occupied by the wife or husband of the governor general, is the governor general's study. On the opposite side of the corridor is the special door that has always been used by a prime minister coming to consult Canada's head of state. If you are invited into the study you will discover a spacious semi-circular room, built in 1906 with panelled walls and lined with bookcases, which is at once a working office and a place to receive visitors. If you look out through the tall windows, you will see the great perennial flower beds, the sweeping lawns, and the trees of Rideau Hall's grounds. Over the fireplace is the royal coat of arms, since the occupant represents the monarchy in Canada. On the walls are oak panels with the names and dates of installation of each governor general who has worked here. The great mahogany desk was made at the time of the Napoleonic wars. Nearby sits a computer.

A Happily Haunted Place

There are really no office hours to being governor general. A lot of work takes place in small meetings or very informal public discussions or formal ceremonies or over meals. Seventy percent of the time we're somewhere else in the country, most often in smaller, more isolated communities, at gatherings in school gyms and community centres. When you are governor general you meet people under specific circumstances: there's a formalized way in which heads of state receive each other. They have private conversations with nobody else present, and then they move on to be joined by others, and then, usually, to eat something together. This is a ritual that's been the same for hundreds of years. It is part of the ongoing, stable relationship between nations.

So many great historical figures have sat in this office and talked to governors general since 1911, when the study was built: Winston Churchill, Charles de Gaulle, Nelson Mandela, John F. Kennedy ... I remember when the Aga Khan, the head of the world's Ismaili Muslim community, came and sat here. We talked about the dramatic exodus of his people from East Africa, and how he had organized with Prime Minister Trudeau for Canada to take in about 10,000 of his people. I was deeply impressed by his assumption of responsibility for them, and his guarantee to Canada that they would not be a charge to the nation.

You can sense their ghosts—not real ones, of course (I've never seen a real one, although I think there probably are a few)—but the spirits of the people who have lived here and talked here, the people whose lives have touched this place. And, of course, I'm surrounded by the names of all my predecessors, which are etched into the frieze running around the top of the wall. I'm conscious that all of them were here. *AC*

Haida ceremonial mask by Steven Mitchell, mounted on a wall in the governor general's study.

BLANC
1995
CLARKSON
1999

One door in the study leads to the elegant room, built in the 1860s, that has always housed the governor general's wife or husband. It has seen many different colours and has been, in turn, a parlour, a boudoir, and now a study. The spouse—Her Excellency in the past but, more recently, His Excellency—has no official appointment but can have enormous influence. Lady Dufferin, for instance, played a key role during the Pacific Scandal that cost Sir John A. Macdonald the 1873 election; Lady Aberdeen was instrumental in establishing the Victorian Order of Nurses, an important step for the women's movement in Canada; Gabrielle Léger helped direct the rebuilding of the burnt-down Citadelle in Quebec City (the governor general's other official residence), while Lily Schreyer worked to win equal treatment for people with disabilities and was a big supporter of the craft industry; Maurice Sauvé oversaw the rebuilding of the kitchens and pantry; Gerda Hnatyshyn collected Canadian furniture for both official residences and worked on a new rose garden (and also found time to write a book about Rideau Hall); Diana Fowler LeBlanc took a keen interest in aboriginal youth and established a scholarship for aboriginal social work (she was also active in promoting palliative care); and John Ralston Saul has worked to strengthen bilingualism and to encourage the study of Canadian history.

The spouses have also helped to make Rideau Hall fun. In 1876 Lady Dufferin gave a fancy dress ball that remained the favourite topic of conversation in Canada for months after.

A Place for Ideas

Rideau Hall has always been a place that welcomes ideas. It has always been a place where, while politics are banished, no topic is out of bounds. Conversations about the nature of Canada have been going on at Rideau Hall since before Confederation because the people who come here were and are involved in shaping the country in every possible way and at every level. So, over the years, most viceregal couples have been actively engaged in the national conversation.

The office I work in has been used by the spouse of the governor general since before Confederation. It's the sunniest, warmest room in the house. It's a room with a wonderful history. It was here that Lady Aberdeen plotted the creation of the Canadian women's movement through the formation of the National Council of Women and the Victorian Order of Nurses (VON): serious work for women, which the doctors saw as unpleasant competition for their power and their income. After dinner, in the smoking room (which no longer exists), the men argued affairs of state over port and cigars, a conversation from which women—even Lady Aberdeen—were excluded. I can imagine her storming about in here wanting to change the world. But even when she was kept behind the scenes, she was making her influence felt. And her successor, Lady Minto, raised the funds for the first forty county health centres in which the VONs worked. *JRS*

Opposite: A campaign poster for Wilfrid Laurier, Canada's first French Canadian prime minister, is one of the personal possessions in John Ralston Saul's study. In front of the portrait are small Buddhas from Thailand and Burma.

"There never was so splendid a ball on this side of the Atlantic," reported the *Canadian Illustrated News*. Court jesters, Marie Antoinettes, Hamlets, Little Bo-Peeps, and Bluebeards crammed together into the new ballroom. On another occasion, when Lady Dufferin stood in for her sick husband at the annual New Year's Day Levee, she reported that "two hundred and seventy came to see me, greeted me, and passed through the drawing-room into the dining-room for tea or champagne—mostly champagne." Today Rideau Hall continues to bring Canadians together to enjoy the best in Canadian food and wine.

Along the corridor is a small space that is known as the May Court Sitting Room. It once hosted the Haddo Club (after a much-loved house in Scotland), founded by the high-minded and determined Lady Aberdeen. The club was open to the whole household, from the Earl of Aberdeen to the cooks, and offered debates, singing and art classes, a study group on Canadian history, French classes, and lectures on important topics by Lady Aberdeen herself. The humourless Lord Minto, successor to Lord Aberdeen, was horrified at the stories he heard of his predecessors' regime. Worst of all, he said, was the Haddo Club, where the butler had once out-argued Lord Aberdeen.

The early inhabitants of Rideau Hall made their own entertainment. Lady Dufferin explained in a letter to her mother that she could not have balls during Lent, but she could have plays. "Two pieces, 'The First Night' and 'To Oblige Benson,' are already in hand, and we are to have one play each week, and each play twice." During her "At Homes," Lady Aberdeen left the ballroom free for dancing but had a quartet playing in her drawing room. When the great singer Nellie Melba discovered that the Rideau Hall staff had not been able to get into her concert in Ottawa, she insisted on doing a special one for them in the Ballroom. One evening Pauline Johnson came to recite some of her poems. "She was dressed in Indian costume," Lady Aberdeen wrote in her journal, "& one of her pieces describing an encounter of an Indian chief with some white settlers, the Indians shot dead & the

Preceding pages: The governor general's study is very much a reflection of its occupant. Among the paintings and furniture from Clarkson's personal collection are *The Arctic Raven*, by Kananginak Pootoogook, and two striking portraits by the Canadian painter Attila Richard Lukacs (*Portraits #6 and #7*). To the right of the works hangs *Haida Woman with Labret* by Joe David, on loan from the Vancouver Art Gallery. The sofas are by Toronto's Christopher Wood and the coffee table with its apples and branches in iron is by Victor Cicansky.

Opposite: A performance in the Ballroom theatre at Rideau Hall in the 1870s. Lord Dufferin is the second man from the right. Lady Dufferin was a great devotée of amateur theatricals. One Christmas she directed a fairy tale for the youngsters. In March of 1875 she produced an operetta whose lyrics were written by her children's tutor to music by the organist at the Ottawa cathedral. "I asked the actors to keep on their costumes during the evening," she wrote, "and they made the party look very gay and pretty, the girls coloured petticoats and high white caps and the men's bright-coloured clothes being very effective."

Overleaf: Children's fancy dress party in the Tent Room, Christmas 1912.

CHILDRENS FANCY DRESS BALL
RIDEAU HALL - 1912.

The Winter Party

The idea of doing a day-long winter party for the public is naturally Canadian. It was Lord and Lady Dufferin, back in the 1870s, who put in the first skating rink and gave the first winter party. (And, of course, Lord Stanley established the most important hockey trophy in 1893.) But those early winter parties were for invited guests only—rather elite affairs. And until recently there was no established tradition of winter parties open to the public, although from time to time public parties were held.

In 2002, to coincide with the fiftieth anniversary of the appointment of the first Canadian governor general, we made the winter party into an annual event open to everyone. Now thousands of Canadians come to the Rideau Hall winter party, not just from Ottawa but from all over the country—and they bring their kids. They bring their skates or their cross-country skis (the sugar bush is opened up to skiers). The more people who come who don't live in Ottawa, the better. There are dog teams and sleds and anyone who wants to can take a ride. Rideau Hall serves refreshments—hot chocolate and cookies—and we do maple syrup taffy pulls on the snow. It's a great time. *AC*

wild lament . . . of the daughter of those who had robbed her people of their land, was v. telling." During his tenure, Lord Tweedsmuir, better known as the writer John Buchan, told ghost stories in the darkened drawing room. "Terrifyingly vivid, blood-chilling ghost stories," remembered an aide-de-camp, "that brought gasps from the adults and sharp squeals from the children."

Many of the visitors from Britain came to love the Canadian winters. "A beautiful, ideal winter day: the ground and trees white with snow, blue sky and sun," wrote Lady Dufferin of her first November in Canada. "The children were unable to resist some of the pleasures of a first day of snow, and tumbled about in it as though it were sand."

Rideau Hall has had skating since 1878. The staff still play shinny after work and the public skates on weekends on what may be the oldest outdoor rink on the continent. At some point in the nineteenth century, someone, perhaps the Swedish governess to the Aberdeen children, introduced skiing. The hills were also good for tobogganing. Lady Aberdeen slid down decorously with her husband but never got used to it. "It leaves too much of one's inside behind one to be comfortable for such folk as me—still it wasn't bad." Nor did she much like the hockey that was sometimes played on the Rideau Hall rinks: "It presents too fierce a temptation for roughness & unfairness for any average person. I am sure that I should murder my opponents if I were to play at such close quarters & with a stick in one's hand." Lord Minto, by contrast, developed such an enthusiasm for hockey that he played in the Rideau Hall pick-up games.

An unidentified skater in front of the ice castle—thin sheets of ice were used for the windows—during the 1880s. The governor general at the time, the Marquess of Lansdowne, was a keen skater, as were his wife and two daughters, one of whom would return to Rideau Hall in 1916 as the Duchess of Devonshire.

The Dufferins built a covered rink for curling—that "sort of billiards on ice," as one visitor described it. When the Lansdownes occupied Rideau Hall in the mid-1880s, a military band sitting in an ice pavilion played at the weekly skating parties. Twice a winter the Lansdownes gave elaborate evening skating and tobogganing parties. The grounds and the rinks were lit with bonfires and Japanese lanterns, and footmen in fur coats and caps served dinner in the curling rink. The tradition started by the Dufferins goes on as an annual public event that now includes cross-country skiing and dog-sled rides.

Rideau Hall has recorded many happy memories. Lord Dufferin kept a skeleton hanging in his study to startle his callers; sometimes there were competitions for the most outlandish costume at dinner. (To this day, on Halloween, the Rideau Hall staff decorate the entrance with pumpkins and dress up as witches, ghosts, and skeletons for the local children, who line up on the long driveway from Sussex Drive to be properly scared.) In 1919 a young war veteran, the shy and awkward Harold Macmillan, was appointed as an aide-de-camp, fell madly in love with the Duke of Devonshire's daughter Dorothy, and left Canada an engaged man. It also has sadder memories. During both world wars, the young aides-de-camp disappeared to fight, in some cases never to return. A maid returning home to Britain in 1915 went down with the *Lusitania*.

Above: A lone skier on Rideau Hall's renowned toboggan run, which ordinarily was populated with a "merry, romping company," to quote one observer. "Put a toboggan and two or three beaux at her disposal," the observer continued, "and a pretty Canadian girl never looks prettier." *Opposite*: A game of curling in the enclosed rink built by Lord Dufferin at his own expense and opened in 1873.

Overleaf: The Athlones' grandchildren (*left to right*), Elizabeth (*head only visible*), Richard, and Anne, who took refuge at Rideau Hall for a time during the Second World War, enjoy the skating rink in the company of two aides-de-camp—the Honourable E. Chatfield (*crouched at left*) and Lt. Dunn Lantier (*centre*)—and Ariel Baird, lady-in-waiting to Princess Alice, the Countess of Athlone, who leads the procession wearing a Hudson's Bay blanket-coat.

CHAPTER 2

A Canadian Symbol And just as there is no one style for heads of state, there is no one style for national houses, which, like their inhabitants, possess both a physical existence and a symbolic one.

A nineteenth-century view of the Parliament Buildings from the Ottawa River. All but the Parliamentary Library (the round building rising to a pointed peak in right mid-ground) were destroyed in the fire of 1916, leaving Rideau Hall as the most important public building to remain intact from the time of Confederation.

Heads of state help their societies to see themselves more clearly, but they also reflect the values of those societies. The Scandinavian monarchs are famously informal; the Japanese emperor is hidden under layers of protocol. Styles change too, over time. Buckingham Palace was built as much to conceal the British monarchs as display them, but today the Queen throws open the State Rooms and the grounds to the paying public as part of an attempt to become more democratic. The American president, in contrast, has become increasingly imperial as the United States has risen to world power. In certain heavily militarized European nations of the 1900s, the heads of state appeared more often than not in uniform; today, in a different Europe, they wear civilian clothes

Even before Confederation, the role of Canada's governor general had evolved from that of the chief executive to something more like a constitutional monarch. The British monarchy itself was already becoming non-partisan and largely symbolic. As Dufferin told a crowd in Halifax in 1873, the governor general "has no political friends, still less need he have political enemies; the possession of either—nay, even to be suspected of possessing either—destroys his usefulness." By the time his term was up, Dufferin had concluded that there was "little scope in the administration of Canada for an ambitious governor general."

In the first decades after Confederation much about the position of the governor general was unclear. He (it was only men in those days) acted at once as the agent of the British government in Canada, the spokesman for Canada to Britain, and the representative of the British Crown. In theory, he exercised great powers, including the right to appoint and dismiss officials, from the prime minister himself to judges, and the right to call and dismiss Parliament. Just as the British monarch had long since relinquished such powers, however, so the Canadian governor general was circumscribed by established practice and by precedent. Since 1848, when responsible government came to the Canadian colonies, governors general have, under one of those frequent conventions of Canadian constitutional history, been expected to accept the advice of their prime ministers in all matters.

There is much disagreement about what makes a country: geography, of course, a functioning government, and perhaps a shared history or values. Everyone knows, without really discussing it, that countries have their own postage stamps, flags, and national anthems. And all countries have heads of state: some, like the American president, with real political power and some who are hereditary monarchs. Other countries' heads of state, among them Canada's governor general, perform a job whose functions are largely ceremonial. (The governor general's influence, which can be considerable, is another matter.) But never discount ceremony; just ask members of the Canadian forces who've served in the Arabian Gulf, where Adrienne Clarkson and John Ralston Saul celebrated Christmas on two Canadian frigates, or in Kabul, where they shared New Year celebrations with our troops stationed there.

The role of head of state is as ancient as human history itself. A head of state symbolizes the nation in good times and bad and performs the duties and conducts the rituals that summon up what we share as citizens. And just as there is no one style for heads of state, there is no one style for national houses, which, like their inhabitants, possess both a physical

La Citadelle

The official residence within the Quebec City Citadelle was originally established by Lord Dufferin as a summer place for the governor general. But we prefer going there in the winter, in February, when the snow is deep—Quebec is a perfect winter city—and everyone is in town and working and we are able to spend time with the community.

The residence, which sits along the cliff above the St. Lawrence River, was formerly the officers' quarters of the fort. And while it is still a grand house, it is much smaller and therefore more homey than Rideau Hall. Being an official residence, it does have a ballroom, and there's a magnificent verandah and terrace with that famous view sweeping up and down the St. Lawrence, which in the winter is a forest of grinding ice.

At the Citadelle you are at the very heart of the history of New France and thus the history of Canada as a country. In the most profound sense, the office of governor general goes straight back to Champlain. In Canada there has always been a "gouverneur" in either Quebec City or Ottawa. The residence has certainly seen more than its share of post-Confederation history. For example, twice during the Second World War Mackenzie King, Churchill, and Roosevelt met in Quebec City and stayed at the Citadelle with the Earl and Countess of Athlone. (We're still trying to figure out who slept in which room.) Some ambassadors present their credentials in Quebec City and we have held important ceremonies there: the Bravery Awards, an Order of Canada investiture, citizenship ceremonies, and a great round table on the Arctic. We do our utmost to make it a place where Quebeckers come together with other Canadians from all over the country, anglophone and francophone. *AC*

Opposite top: An early twentieth-century view of Quebec City. The chimneys of the Citadelle residence are visible behind the fortress wall high on the left. *Opposite below*: Lady Aberdeen and Lord Aberdeen (*centre*) pose with Prime Minister Sir Wilfrid Laurier (who is at Lord Aberdeen's left) at the Citadelle in 1898.

existence and a symbolic one. Consider India when it was the jewel in the crown of the British Empire. In the 1920s Sir Edwin Lutyens built a magnificent imperial capital in New Delhi with a massive viceregal palace to symbolize "the ideal and fact of British rule in India." British rule has long vanished in India, and Rashtrapati Bhavan, as it now is, symbolizes the independent state of India. Think of Russia and you think of the Kremlin—even when the Communists broke with the Tsarist past, they could not resist turning a former royal palace into the heart of Soviet government. Those domes and spires, those high walls enclosing a jumble of buildings from centuries past, say something about Russia's turbulent and tragic history. Or think of the Elysée Palace. Once home to Mme de Pompadour, mistress to Louis XV, later to one of Napoleon's marshals, and now to the French president, it was erected when France dominated Europe militarily and culturally. Its great ceremonial courtyard and its magnificent apartments were designed to impress—and they still do.

Look south, as we often do in Canada, to Washington and the White House. George Washington wanted a new capital for a new country, one laid out on rational lines. The president's house, dignified and elegant, suitable for a gentleman rather than a monarch, expressed much about the hopes of the new country. When the British burned it to the ground in 1812, its rebuilding—exactly as it had looked before—became part of the American determination to survive and triumph. The White House, as its official Web site proudly says, "has stood as a symbol of the Presidency, the United States government, and the American people." Compared with

Constitutionally Canadian

In 1848, when Lord Elgin called on Louis-Hippolyte LaFontaine to form Canada's first properly responsible government, he put together the two essential halves of a democracy: a reasonably broad electorate and a government controlled by the elected legislature—not a small and wealthy elite or the governor general or the British ministry.

Forget the technical niceties (Canadians take decades to work these things out). From 1848 on, the governor general was expected to act to defend the legitimacy of our democracy; the Crown became the guarantor of Canadian responsible government. So, whether governors general were British or Canadian, they were expected to act as if they were Canadians. In a broader sense, their job was to advance Canadian civilization, Canadian values, Canadian interests—not British ones. Ironically, many of the early British-born governors general (many of whom were themselves bilingual) understood the essentials of our civilization—for example, the bilingual nature of the country and the role of aboriginal people—

better and supported them more enthusiastically than our home-grown elites.

Once the governor general had given up his executive power, the office had to be reinvented. And it was Lord and Lady Elgin who really established the concept of the viceregal couple. In the absence of a central political role, they took the office in the direction of advancing Canadian culture.

When I talk to visitors to Rideau Hall, I always tell them that traces of the Canadian experiment in responsible government are in this house. Every government since Confederation has been sworn in here. Every one of Canada's great initiatives as well as every one of our deepest crises has been discussed in private between the governor general and the prime minister. Everywhere you walk in this house, you are walking where Macdonald and Laurier and all of their successors have walked or danced, or drunk! And because the Centre Block of Parliament burned down during the First World War, Rideau Hall is the only public building that has seen and heard them all. *JRS*

countries in Europe and with the United States, Canada's path to nationhood has been slower and gentler. We have had no transformative act of rebellion, no violent overthrowing of the past. Canada has grown gradually as a nation, from the first encounters between the First Nations and the Europeans through the settlement of New France and the British conquest. And we have gained our independence incrementally. In the nineteenth century we were proud—at least much of English Canada was—to be part of the British Empire, at the time the greatest power in the world. In the twentieth century we took a leading role in turning it into the Commonwealth of Nations. Rideau Hall has had a quieter, less dramatic evolution than some other official residences. The Australians, whose history followed a similar evolution, also converted a private house into the governor general's official residence. Yarralumla, in Canberra, was built in the same decade as Rideau Hall to be the hunting lodge of a prosperous civil servant. It too has changed almost out of recognition. In 1913 the Australian government bought the house, and it has been tinkering with it ever since, just as it has with Australia's constitution.

The talk of tearing down Rideau Hall and starting over has long faded away. While there have often been complaints about the house's awkward nooks and crannies, the costs of its repairs and maintenance, it too stands today for a different country than it once did. The portraits of the governors general that hang on its walls move from men in the formal dress of the nineteenth and early twentieth centuries to more modern figures in pullovers or sports jackets. The English lords and royal princes give way to the men, and eventually to the women, who have been appointed, in effect, heads of state of Canada. And where the Elgins and Dufferins presided over a country inhabited mostly by people of aborginal, French, and British stock, Edward Schreyer, Jeanne Sauvé, Ramon Hnatyshyn, Roméo LeBlanc, and Adrienne Clarkson have looked out on a country whose people come from just about every corner of the globe.

From 1916 on, when Prime Minister Sir Robert Borden protested that he had not been consulted in the appointment of Victor Cavendish (Duke of Devonshire) as governor general, the British government deferred to Canadian wishes in the selection. In 1921 the Canadian choice was Julian Byng, already famous as the British commander when Canadian troops successfully stormed Vimy Ridge during the First World War. Brisk, direct, and eccentric (his aides despaired as he wandered about Ottawa on his own in a frayed hat and old rubber boots), Lord Byng was comfortable with Canadians of all backgrounds. But even governors general who had first served elsewhere in the British Empire—Lord Willingdon, for example, or the Earl of Athlone—understood that, once appointed, they now represented Canada. After the Statute of Westminster of 1931 made Canada autonomous within the Commonwealth, the Canadian government took the initiative in letting London know whom it would find acceptable.

Above: Governor General Vincent Massey, wearing the traditional viceregal uniform, congratulates Prime Minister John Diefenbaker at the swearing in of his cabinet after the 1957 election. *Opposite*: Prince Philip and Queen Elizabeth II seem more interested in the governor general's dog, Duff (short for Dufferin), who is carrying the Queen's handbag, than in the viceregent himself, in this famous 1957 photo.

After the Second World War, Prime Minister William Lyon Mackenzie King toyed briefly with the idea of nominating General Andrew McNaughton, who served with distinction in the First World War and commanded Canada's overseas forces in the Second, to succeed Athlone, but in the end he decided the time for a Canadian had not yet come. So the last of the British governors general was a distinguished general from that war, Viscount Alexander of Tunis. In 1952, however, King's successor, Louis St. Laurent, submitted only one name to Buckingham Palace for approval: Vincent Massey.

It is hard to imagine a better transitional figure. Educated at the University of Toronto and at Oxford, Massey was at once Canadian and British. He was devoted equally to Canada

and to the British Crown. He moved as easily in Liberal circles in Canada as he did in British society. And Canadians were secretly proud of the story that an upper-class Englishman had once complained: "Damn it all, the fellow always makes one feel like a bloody savage." Shortly before his appointment he had presided over the Royal Commission on National Development in the Arts, Letters and Sciences, which laid the intellectual foundations of Canadian cultural policy and led to the creation of the Canada Council and of the National Library. As governor general he created the Governor General's Awards for Architecture and established the Massey Medal to recognize achievement in Canadian geography.

Massey also took an active interest in improving the state of Rideau Hall and its furnishings, which included, in his words, "some of the most regrettable pieces of furniture I have ever seen." He worked closely with the Department of Public Works to repair and refurbish the house. From his time up to the present, the Canadian government has taken a more direct hand in looking after the buildings and grounds, and in a more systematic way. It is not an easy job: only the long-suffering building managers have any idea of what lies behind the walls and under the floorboards.

To Canadianize with Meaning

It's one thing to modernize, to Canadianize, it's quite another to do so within a framework that gives meaning. If all you're doing is putting in new furniture or paintings or curtains because they're Canadian, it may be better or worse, but that doesn't make it more interesting. It becomes more interesting when people can sense that these objects belong together and why. When the Rideau Hall guides take people around, they try to explain what they are seeing, the historic meaning, the artistic meaning, the social meaning. So when they look at the paintings by Jean-Paul Riopelle or Paul-Émile Borduas, they learn that they are looking at images that emerged out of a movement called Le Refus Global, which contributed to the modernization of French Canada. So they're not just looking at great paintings, they're looking into a profound social drama in Canada's history. Or take the two very different Lawren Harris paintings, an archetypal Arctic landscape and a subtly disturbing painting of a Toronto slum. When you consider the two paintings together, you realize they are the work of someone who understood the complex nature of Canada.

The mix of furniture and other objects here now reflects the country—the people who came and settled here and became part of the Canadian story. I'm very proud of those things. And into that mix we've been able to put great paintings loaned from public museums and galleries right across the country as well as from the Canada Council Art Bank.

Even if Rideau Hall's contents could fill a very interesting museum, it isn't a museum. It's one thing to go to a public gallery and look at picture after picture, or room after room, say of the Group of Seven; it's a scholarly approach to art, and it's valuable. But for people who just want to enjoy art without being intimidated, it helps to see it in a domestic context, which is what most art was originally intended for. *AC*

At the foot of the viceregal staircase hangs Alex Colville's *Woman at Clothesline* (1957), which is on loan from the National Gallery of Canada.

Government House as a piece of architecture might be regarded as possessing a certain lovable eccentricity . . . Perhaps the fact that it was originally a private house gave it the basic character of a home which it has never lost.

VINCENT MASSEY

Opposite top: Canoe stories and songs being performed during the Governor General's Party in the Garden, June 30, 2004. The event had storytelling and songs by some of Canada's best-known canoeists and wilderness adventurers, including James Raffan (*standing*), the storyteller here. *Opposite below*: Some of the thousands of picnickers who crowded the grounds of Rideau Hall for the annual Party in the Garden. The annual summer concert series was launched on the same day with performances by Shaye and Spirit of the West.

Before the last few decades, decorating at Rideau Hall was done in a hit-and-miss way, depending on personal taste and the fashion of the time. Governors general still bring their own style to Rideau Hall, and private individuals and other governments still donate to the house. The National Capital Commission and the Canadiana Fund (which is supported by donations from private individuals and hunts out the best in Canadian furniture) are its long-term guardians. The Commission's desire to restore some rooms to the period in which they were first built has raised tricky questions. What was the original colour on the walls? What colours are authentic to the period?

But Rideau Hall has always been a Canadian house. It did not suddenly change when Canadians started presiding there. Even in the days when the British governors general and their families came from Britain for their appointed terms with their own belongings, the cold Canadian air still seeped in under the doors and the humid summer heat was just as stifling. Thomas MacKay used a European model for his country estate, but he built it from local materials. Rideau Hall's chefs used to come from Europe, but they depended on Canadian trout and quail. The governors general in the years immediately following Confederation always bought many of the furnishings locally, although the results—the Willingdons' stuffed grizzly bear in the entrance hall with a tray for vistors' cards, for example—were not always happy.

Even in the late nineteenth and early twentieth centuries, when rules and precedents and procedures hemmed the governor general about, Rideau Hall was always more open than Government House in India, for instance, where the distance between rulers and ruled was vast. The most formal occasions had a Canadian flavour. "Guests and waiters chatting to each other seemed a little odd at first," recalled a steward to the Duke of Connaught, "but we soon got used to this and thoroughly enjoyed waiting." There are many echoes of the past in Rideau Hall today, just as there are in Canada itself. Military bands still play on the grounds but there are also huge free concerts with performers like Gordon Lightfoot, Jeff Healey's

The Pauline Vanier Room

The job of Rideau Hall is to project Canada to Canadians and to visitors from other countries. Once the Canadian-born governors general came in, they gradually began to put a more Canadian face on the house. Under Georges and Pauline Vanier, the house was still in transition from the British period to the Canadian period, and one of the significant moments was Pauline Vanier identifying a single room, which was actually part of the original 1830s house, to become the Canadian Room. In it she started gathering a collection of early, mainly Lower Canadian, furniture—very beautiful furniture—including one of the finest late-eighteenth-century armoires in the country. (It has its original paint and a little mouse hole; armoires were often used to store food.)

Madame Vanier's initiative tells you something of the mentality of the time. In what was essentially an English house, the wife of the second Canadian-born governor general set aside a single room to show off historic Canadian furniture.

Recently, one of the Rideau Hall program officers, Adam Barratt, commented, "I don't know why we still call this the Canadian Room, because the whole house is Canadian now!" The evolution has taken four decades, but the idea now is that the furniture, whether it's modern or old, must be Canadian; the paintings are among the finest Canadian works anywhere; the objects in the rooms are Canadian; the themes are Canadian (as is the food and the wine). Because this is our national house, it should be a place to show off the whole of Canada.

So it's no longer the Canadian Room. We've renamed it the Pauline Vanier room in honour of the woman who started the process. It was also a recognition, immediately understood by everybody who knows the house, that we are in a new era, an era in which Rideau Hall is in all possible ways Canada's House. *JRS*

Jazz Wizards, and Natalie MacMaster attracting up to 15,000 people five or six times a summer. The guests no longer wear flowered hats or summer suits, but now sport mostly T-shirts and shorts.

As Canada reached maturity and as Canadians became more self-confident, Rideau Hall came to be seen as a showcase of Canadian culture as well as an official residence. Pauline Vanier started consciously collecting Canadian furniture in the 1950s and decided to convert what was once a smoking room for the governor general's aides into a Canadian collection. She had the room panelled in the folksy knotty pine so popular for basement recreation rooms all across the Canada of the 1950s. The panelling has been covered over, but successive viceregal couples have turned the room into a treasure trove of Canadian paintings and aboriginal sculptures, simple rough-hewn pine tables and sideboards, and elaborate furniture in walnut and maple from Quebec in the style of eighteenth-century France. The largest hooked rug in Canada, with all the provincial and territorial flowers, lies on the floor—Roméo LeBlanc got Acadian artisans in Chéticamp, Cape Breton, to make it. The rocking chair was made in New Brunswick and given to the Hnatyshyns in 1990. A rare cupboard from a Ukrainian Catholic church in Manitoba stands near one corner; although it is carved and painted, one side remains bare, in keeping with the traditions of the church.

A nineteenth-century church pulpit panel from Grosse-Île, Quebec, where thousands of immigrants waited to be admitted into North America. The fleur-de-lys on the left symbolizes French Canadians welcoming new immigrants on the right.

That mix of styles and periods gives Rideau Hall much of its distinctive charm. The contents of the house have drifted in over the decades and from all over the world. Like Canada itself, Rideau Hall has brought together many different traditions. And it continues to do so; recent acquisitions range from a stylized aboriginal mask made by an artist from Paulatuk, NWT, to a 2,000-year-old Chinese bronze. Victorian landscapes hang beside boldly modernist ones; sleek modern consoles made in Canada stand next to Elizabethan chairs. In the Ballroom an enormous crystal chandelier, donated by the British government to thank Canada for its participation in the Second World War, shines down on the colours of the vanished Canadian Guards regiment, on stained-glass windows commissioned by the Hnatyshyns, and on Jean-Paul Lemieux's gently satirical portrait of Queen Elizabeth and Prince Philip. The spouses have taken a hand in Rideau Hall's refurbishings: Norah Michener collected paintings and photographs of her predecessors, while Gabrielle Léger added works by modern Canadian artists and, with her husband, chose Lemieux to paint their portrait.

Above: The Ballroom's neo-classical crystal chandelier has 12,000 pieces of Waterford crystal and eighty light bulbs, and weighs in at one imperial ton. *Opposite*: *La Reine et le Duc d'Edimbourg* (1979) by Jean-Paul Lemieux portrays the royal couple in an idealized field of flowers with the Parliament Buildings in the background. The room's Chippendale-style chairs from the turn of the century harmonize with the décor of the Ballroom, which has recently been restored to its original colours. AC: "I was in the Basilica in Quebec City for a memorial service a year after 9/11, when it struck me that the carved wooden pillars in the magnificent choir were exactly like the ones in the Ballroom at Rideau Hall. I'm sure the pillars are the work of the same craftsmen—after all, Lord Dufferin loved Quebec City so much and spent so much time there."

Rideau Hall is at once a lived-in house, a gallery of Canadian arts and crafts, and a museum of Canadian history, but it is also, as Massey put it, "an instrument for Canada." His main responsibility as governor general, he believed, was to bring Canadians together on neutral ground. And Rideau Hall could do this by "dispensing hospitality" in a way that combines "dignity and warmth." Its hospitality is on a demanding scale, perhaps more than ever before: during her term of office, Adrienne Clarkson served some 60,000 meals a year. Rideau Hall reaches out to Canadians in so many ways. Governors general have always travelled, by carriage, canoe, dogsled, train, car, airplane, and boat, to every part of Canada to meet Canadians where they live. They visit schools and orphanages and open hospitals or take part in aboriginal healing circles or traditional feasts.

The house at its best has aspired to bridge divisions among Canadians in the name of a common nation. Be careful in giving out invitations, the confidential manual for Rideau

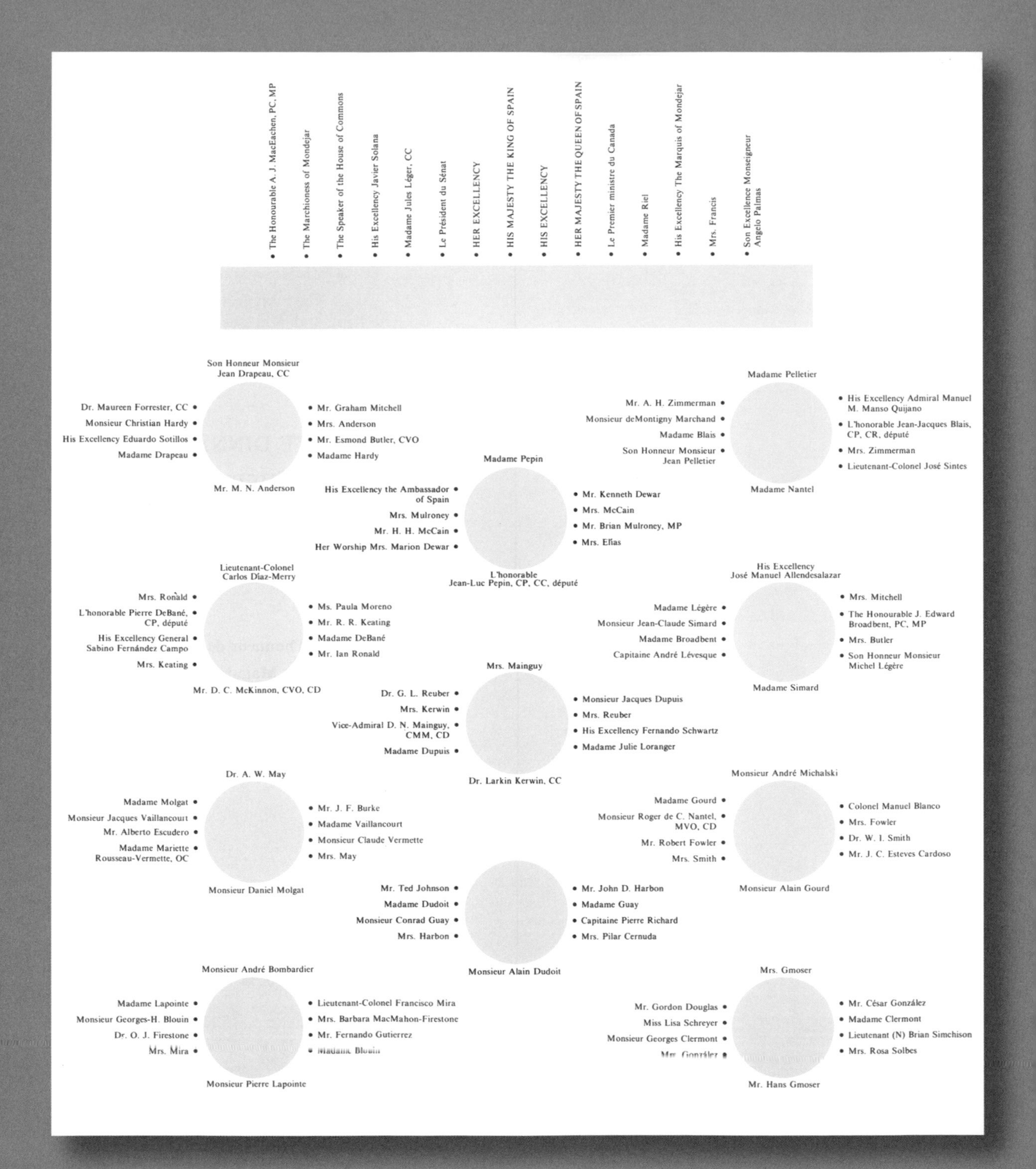

The Honourable A. J. MacEachen, PC, MP
The Marchioness of Mondejar
The Speaker of the House of Commons
His Excellency Javier Solana
Madame Jules Léger, CC
Le Président du Sénat
HER EXCELLENCY
HIS MAJESTY THE KING OF SPAIN
HIS EXCELLENCY
HER MAJESTY THE QUEEN OF SPAIN
Le Premier ministre du Canada
Madame Riel
His Excellency The Marquis of Mondejar
Mrs. Francis
Son Excellence Monseigneur Angelo Palmas
Son Honneur Monsieur Jean Drapeau, CC
Dr. Maureen Forrester, CC
Monsieur Christian Hardy
His Excellency Eduardo Sotillos
Madame Drapeau
Mr. Graham Mitchell
Mrs. Anderson
Mr. Esmond Butler, CVO
Madame Hardy
Mr. M. N. Anderson
Madame Pelletier
Mr. A. H. Zimmerman
Monsieur deMontigny Marchand
Madame Blais
Son Honneur Monsieur Jean Pelletier
His Excellency Admiral Manuel M. Manso Quijano
L'honorable Jean-Jacques Blais, CP, CR, député
Mrs. Zimmerman
Lieutenant-Colonel José Sintes
Madame Nantel
Madame Pepin
His Excellency the Ambassador of Spain
Mrs. Mulroney
Mr. H. H. McCain
Her Worship Mrs. Marion Dewar
Mr. Kenneth Dewar
Mrs. McCain
Mr. Brian Mulroney, MP
Mrs. Elías
L'honorable Jean-Luc Pepin, CP, CC, député
Lieutenant-Colonel Carlos Díaz-Merry
Mrs. Ronald
L'honorable Pierre DeBané, CP, député
His Excellency General Sabino Fernández Campo
Mrs. Keating
Ms. Paula Moreno
Mr. R. R. Keating
Madame DeBané
Mr. Ian Ronald
Mr. D. C. McKinnon, CVO, CD
His Excellency José Manuel Allendesalazar
Madame Légère
Monsieur Jean-Claude Simard
Madame Broadbent
Capitaine André Lévesque
Mrs. Mitchell
The Honourable J. Edward Broadbent, PC, MP
Mrs. Butler
Son Honneur Monsieur Michel Légère
Madame Simard
Mrs. Mainguy
Dr. G. L. Reuber
Mrs. Kerwin
Vice-Admiral D. N. Mainguy, CMM, CD
Madame Dupuis
Monsieur Jacques Dupuis
Mrs. Reuber
His Excellency Fernando Schwartz
Madame Julie Loranger
Dr. Larkin Kerwin, CC
Dr. A. W. May
Madame Molgat
Monsieur Jacques Vaillancourt
Mr. Alberto Escudero
Madame Mariette Rousseau-Vermette, OC
Mr. J. F. Burke
Madame Vaillancourt
Monsieur Claude Vermette
Mrs. May
Monsieur Daniel Molgat
Monsieur André Michalski
Madame Gourd
Monsieur Roger de C. Nantel, MVO, CD
Mr. Robert Fowler
Mrs. Smith
Colonel Manuel Blanco
Mrs. Fowler
Dr. W. I. Smith
Mr. J. C. Esteves Cardoso
Monsieur Alain Gourd
Mr. Ted Johnson
Madame Dudoit
Monsieur Conrad Guay
Mrs. Harbon
Mr. John D. Harbon
Madame Guay
Capitaine Pierre Richard
Mrs. Pilar Cernuda
Monsieur Alain Dudoit
Monsieur André Bombardier
Madame Lapointe
Monsieur Georges-H. Blouin
Dr. O. J. Firestone
Mrs. Mira
Lieutenant-Colonel Francisco Mira
Mrs. Barbara MacMahon-Firestone
Mr. Fernando Gutierrez
Monsieur Pierre Lapointe
Mrs. Gmoser
Mr. Gordon Douglas
Miss Lisa Schreyer
Monsieur Georges Clermont
Mr. César González
Madame Clermont
Lieutenant (N) Brian Simchison
Mrs. Rosa Solbes
Mr. Hans Gmoser

Formal Informalities

Even a state dinner where everyone is dressed in evening clothes doesn't have to be stuffy. Within the essential formal structure of an official function, you can do all sorts of things to enrich the experience. You can even make things up on the spur of the moment. I remember at an Order of Canada dinner when we suddenly realized that we were in the company of all these extraordinary people, but we were the only ones who were expected to get up and speak. Which seemed all wrong. So, during the main course, we asked a few people if they would get up and say a few words—just for three or four minutes—about a person who was an important influence on them or an event that made a profound difference in their lives.

The first time we did this, one of the people we asked to get up was Dorothy Wetherald Rungeling. She was the first woman to become a commercial airline pilot in Canada and was the first Canadian woman to fly a helicopter solo. She's now in her nineties. When Dorothy spoke she told us all how, for some reason, from the time she was a very small girl she just wanted to fly, so she did; there was no stopping her. She was very funny about it, completely unimpressed with herself. Another time one of the people we asked to speak was Daurene E. Lewis, who had become the first black woman mayor in North America. She is the descendent of Black Loyalist refugees who settled in Annapolis Royal in 1783. She'd been a nurse and an entrepreneur and is an educator and a tireless volunteer. She spoke very movingly about her life and then, at the end, she simply said, "Well, I've run out of things to say, so I'm going to sing." And she did. She sang a jubilee called "Castle on the River Nile" very beautifully. That's the sort of thing that happens when you treat a formal event as, above all, a human event. *AC*

A seating plan for the March 12, 1984, state dinner for King Juan Carlos and Queen Sofia of Spain, hosted by Governor General Edward Schreyer and Her Excellency Lily Schreyer.

Hall warned in the 1930s, to share them out equally among the political parties, the different churches, and French- and English-speakers. "It should never be possible for the criticism to be made that any one category of people is favourised or that any one category is neglected." In the Depression 1930s, John Buchan tried to reach out to all Canadians, from the old established settler groups to the new arrivals, and from business elites to farmers and labour leaders. He invited what Ottawa considered dangerous radicals to Rideau Hall: agrarian populists and young socialists from the Co-operative Commonwealth Federation.

There has been much in our short history to divide Canadians: the sheer size of the land, the thinness of our population, our religious and ethnic differences. Buchan was not the only governor general to worry that "each Province tends to regard itself as a separate unit and to look at a policy on the narrowest grounds, without any consideration of Canada as a whole." And, like so many of the others, he worried in particular about the gulf between English- and French-speakers. Lady Aberdeen, ever thorough, engaged a French tutor for the family as soon as she arrived in Canada, as well as a dancing master to show them all Canadian dances. Fifty years later, Massey asked a friend to spend two weeks with him at Rideau Hall to brush up his French. He made a point of speaking in French whenever possible. And, as a French-Canadian intellectual said approvingly, "*On lit Proust à Rideau Hall.*" The appointment of Georges Vanier as the second Canadian-born governor general, a man who came on his father's side from one of the earliest French settlers in Canada and on his mother's from an Irish family, was a reminder of the centrality of the French presence in Canada. Where it was once useful for governors general to be bilingual, recent history has shown that it is now essential.

As the political role of the office of governor general has diminished, its importance to the Canadian nation has grown, especially as a champion of culture: fine art and folk art; writing and publishing; the performing arts in all their guises. The pomp too remains important. We need to celebrate both the diversity of Canadians and the links that join us. We need to commemorate the best that we do, whether in the arts or science, business or volunteer work. Living as we do in the shadow of the United States, with our economy more intertwined with its affairs than ever before, it often seems that the dynamic cultural industries of our southern neighbour are irresistible. In this situation, the governor general helps remind us of who we are. John Buchan launched the Governor General's Literary Awards in 1937 to foster an awareness of the best in Canadian literature.

British though they were, many of our early governors general used their office to encourage the flowering of artistic

Young People at the Nation's House

We both love it when there are young people at Rideau Hall. And one of our most successful gatherings of young Canadians was the Governor General's Youth Forum held in February 2002, when we brought together 101 students from across the country—senior high school students—to talk about leadership. They formed an extraordinary group that reflected every part of the country. The conference lasted four days and ended with an open discussion that was carried live on Newsworld.

At first the students were shy, but pretty soon they relaxed into it. We broke them up into groups that dispersed to all the different rooms of Rideau Hall. Before long they had taken over the house and were treating it the way any teenagers would any place where they feel comfortable. They talked and ate and wandered about. Most of all they talked. The success of French immersion programs across the country could be seen clearly in the young people from Saskatchewan, Alberta, British Columbia, and the Yukon who surprised the francophones by speaking French with them. It inspired the francophones, they said, to learn English!

So, for four days, 101 teenagers took over Rideau Hall. It gave them a real sense of belonging to something bigger than their town or region, a sense of being part of a national community. It certainly blew apart any sense of alienation. And it could happen here because Rideau Hall is so big and because it's the national house, a place where you can pull people together in all sorts of meaningful ways. *AC*

Four of the winners of the Governor General's Literary Awards now on the bookshelves of the governor general's study: bp Nichol (English poetry, 1970); Mordecai Richler (English fiction, 1971); Christopher Moore (English non-fiction, 1982); and Bruce Hutchison (English non-fiction, 1967).

and intellectual life. In 1882 the Marquess of Lorne inaugurated the Royal Society of Canada to bring together leading men of letters, in spite of carping from the *Globe,* which talked of "a mutual admiration society of nincompoops." He hoped, he said in his address, to create a centre of thought and scholarship for all Canadians. He also helped to found a Canadian Academy of Arts to develop Canadian artists. Canada had so many wonderful subjects, he told an audience in Montreal, in its people but also its land. Think of the "magnificent wealth of water in its great streams; in the foaming rush of their cascades, overhung by the mighty pines or branching maples, and skirted with the scented cedar copses." One day, he promised, Canadian artists would make the beauty of Canadian landscapes as well known as any in Europe.

Lord Minto, who was horrified to see historical documents rotting away in dusty piles, persuaded Prime Minister Wilfrid Laurier to appoint a Dominion archivist and then to build a proper public archives, believing that if we do not commemorate our past we cannot know ourselves. He also prevailed upon Laurier to make the Plains of Abraham a national memorial, and urged the government to create national parks to preserve the Canadian wilderness. In 1908 Earl Grey

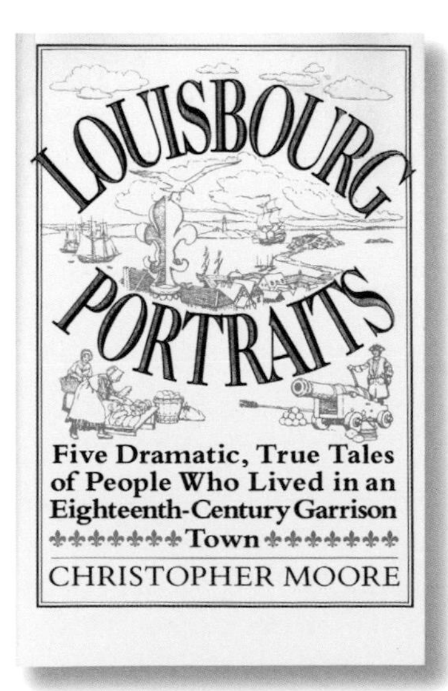

organized elaborate ceremonies to celebrate the tercentenary of the founding of Quebec. The highlight was a historical pageant that culminated with French- and English-speaking soldiers marching side by side while singing "O Canada." And during his time at Rideau Hall, Lord Byng held huge dinners for First World War veterans. That great tradition of cultivating Canadian culture remains alive at Rideau Hall. Massey held a highly successful "writers" weekend, for example, where he brought opinion-makers from all over Canada (men only in those days) to meet each other and interested members of parliament. "They represented every shade of opinion," Massey wrote, "all schools of thought (Conservative, Liberal, socialist, Social Credit, independent, French-Canadian nationalist, and so on)—editors, professors, free-lance journalists, men of letters." He made sure that there was no publicity and that the whole event was informal. "Unusual groupings of people could be seen after dinner, taking Canada to pieces and putting it together again, well into the small hours of the morning." The talking goes on; recently Rideau Hall held a youth forum for sixteen-to-eighteen-year-olds on the future of the country. It also saw a celebration of Pierre Berton's eightieth birthday. Jules and Gabrielle Léger were great supporters of the visual arts and of contemporary music. More recently, Ramon Hnatyshyn established the Governor General's Performing Arts Awards, and Roméo LeBlanc the Governor General's Awards for Visual and Media Arts.

Above: Medal of the Companion of the Order of Canada, designed by Bruce Beatty—who has been in attendance at every Order of Canada investiture since 1967—in the shape of a stylized snowflake and bearing the Latin legend *Desiderantes Meliorem Patriam* ("They desire a better country"). *Opposite below*: Governor General Roland Michener invests legendary hockey player Maurice "Rocket" Richard as an Officer in the Order of Canada in November 1967, the year the award was established. (Michener was the first person to receive the order.)

The important ceremonies at Rideau Hall honour, as they have done for generations, Canadians from all corners of the country—for bravery, for achievements in the arts and sciences, or for contributions to Canadian public life. An Order of Canada investiture is a deeply moving occasion as Canadians of different ages and colours and backgrounds receive their insignia. Some have made great discoveries in medicine; others have worked in obscurity for years to feed hungry schoolchildren. Some have entertained us; others have educated or inspired us. And the names are aboriginal, Vietnamese, English, Ukrainian, French, Chinese, Somali, and more. It is tempting to see symbols in Rideau Hall, and easy to read too

Overleaf left page: This portrait of Adrienne Clarkson, age two, in an antique frame is among the personal items on John Ralston Saul's desk. *Overleaf right page:* Thanks to recent searches in book fairs and second-hand bookstores, the bookshelves in the governor general's study now hold all but two of the past winners of the Governor General's Literary Awards.

Our Canadian culture cannot be a copy of any one old thing—it must be a new thing created by the contributions of all the elements that make up the nation.

JOHN BUCHAN

much into it: to see it as the shrine in which the flame of Canadian nationalism burns or to find in its rambling rooms the soul of the Canadian people. Or to elevate the governor general to the keeper of that flame, the saviour of that soul, the defender of the nation against—well, who? The siren songs from the south? the world? our own tendencies to bicker and quarrel? If Rideau Hall were pulled down tomorrow, Canada would not fail—but it would be diminished. It would lose a part of its past, and without a past we are less as a nation. It would lose an institution that has never stood for a single party, class, region, or interest group but solely for Canada. A hundred years from now the house will probably look different, perhaps with a slightly altered shape and with new colours on the walls, but, if we are fortunate, it will still be carrying out the same job for all Canadians.

WATER

PART 2

In a Canadian Garden.

The Rideau Hall garden is the complete twenty-first-century Canadian garden. We'd like to think that the gardens at Rideau Hall send a very strong message about who we are as a people at the beginning of the twenty-first century. A garden is a place where human beings lay out their vision of nature, their relationship to the natural world.

by Marjorie Harris

CHAPTER I

The Garden in Winter The early gardeners at Rideau Hall waged war against the Canadian climate, planting flowers that looked spectacular in summer but left empty spaces during their winter dormancy.

Above: A winter view looking east over the formal gardens from the steps of the glassed-in Verandah.

Preceding pages: Bearded iris and *Penstemon* provide seamless layers of colour in the new perennial garden on the upper terrace.

The Garden Laid Bare

Winter reveals the bones of a garden. As the snow drifts down around Rideau Hall, a glimpse from any of its dozens of south-facing windows reveals what an astonishing garden this house has. The ornamental beds are still flush with the memory of autumn, and the classic lines first laid out when the original house was built in the 1830s are at once obvious and pleasing. This is a rare nineteenth-century garden surviving pretty much intact into the twenty-first century, yet its most recent renovations have placed it among Canada's leading contemporary gardens. If the underlying skeleton of a garden is strong, then it can withstand a century and a half of tinkering.

The main garden consists of two large consecutive squares running along the south side of the house and the attached greenhouses at the eastern end. The smaller of these, known as the upper terrace, occupies the sheltered corner created by the southwest wing of the building. From the upper terrace, stone steps lead down through a rockery to the much larger lower terrace. To the south of these formal gardens extends a well-treed area dominated by a huge red oak, then a dense wooded area underplanted with hostas, and then an open park space ideal for a croquet pitch, and finally, behind a high hedge, the tennis courts. From here, on summer evenings, the soft thunk of a ball can be heard in the garden.

The upper terrace, which can be entered from the house through a small porch, is the more intimate of these two garden rooms, or self-contained garden areas. It is dominated by a large half-moon-shaped flower bed, which covers almost half the area. A graceful flagstone path winds through the bed to a central patio. And although this bed reaches its peak in summer, the ornamental grasses keep their shape in winter, while the perennials are still heavy with seeds attractive to winter birds. And along the upper garden's perimeter wide beds, or borders—filled with a combination of mature trees, small shrubs, and perennials in dazzling combinations—give shape and provide colour all winter long.

Thinking about Roots

In all times and cultures gardens have been places where people went for peace and reflection, where they set aside for a while the demands of their busy lives. That makes gardens all the more important in today's speeded-up world.

The gardens and grounds at Rideau Hall, which are open to all Canadians, are a good place to reflect on roots—the roots of this historic place and the roots of Canada as a country. The roots of Rideau Hall go back to the mid-nineteenth century, but the place really acquired its essential shape—the shape it maintains to this day—during the early days after Confederation, when the estate was laid out on a Romantic English model. England was an extremely domesticated place, and the great English landscape architects wanted to introduce into their overly certain society some uncertainty—the uncertainty of nature, of wildness. But Canada was not a densely populated, overly domesticated country. Here the wilderness was and is always right at the edges of our lives. In Ottawa, just dig down a foot or two and you hit the Canadian Shield. So what had been a Romantic idea in England was in Canada the reality of the place. As a result, the English model evolved into something quite different here.

Those Victorian governors general laid a good foundation. Much of the work in recent years has been about uncovering that foundation and building on the experience of another hundred years of gardening in Canada. The Rideau Hall grounds are a beautiful and healthy mix of formality and informality with an underlying sense of order and proportion. Which seems like the Canadian way. *AC*

Opposite top: Even in winter, the Norah Michener Rockery (on either side of the steps) beautifully enhances the transition from the upper terrace to the lower terrace. (The glassed-in Verandah, where breakfasts and informal lunches are served, is in the background.) *Opposite below*: Under a thick blanket of snow the dramatic grasses on the lower terrace hold their shape and the woody plants help define the space.

The rockery created by Norah Michener in the 1960s takes us from the upper to the lower terrace, an extensive lawn edged on all four sides with 3-metre-deep ornamental borders. The path that leads from the sunroom of the house and down the steps through the rockery bisects the lower terrace and ends at the rock garden created by Lady Evelyn Byng in the 1920s. If the upper terrace feels intimate, the lower terrace is on a grand scale—a magnificent formal garden, with huge beds enlivened year round by dwarf fruit trees, large shrubs, and giant grasses. Adrienne Clarkson's addition of ornamental grasses was a daring move in such a formal garden and has brought to it a spectacular wild look in winter, especially after a clinging snow gives solidity to their forms.

Just to the south of the upper terrace, beneath stately old maple and oak trees, lies the new woodland garden, which in winter is hidden beneath the snow. And adjacent to the greenhouse attached to the eastern end of the house is the hedged-in kitchen garden. These are the Rideau Hall gardens today, gardens with a wonderful story to tell.

The early gardeners at Rideau Hall waged war against the Canadian climate, planting traditional English herbaceous borders and masses of peonies and phlox—flowers that looked spectacular in summer but left empty spaces during their winter dormancy. However, generations of gardeners, good and bad, have failed to erase what the first owner of Rideau Hall laid out. Good bones make great gardens.

The practice at Rideau Hall is to leave most plants standing at the end of the growing season for animal forage and visual pleasure. With each snowfall these plants change shape. Here, ornamental grasses (*opposite*), grapes left on the vine (*above*), and fat red rosehips (*above right*) create their own unique winter sculptures.

A Northern Site

As with so many Canadian gardens, this one sits in a landscape sculpted during the last Ice Age when seven-storey-high glaciers scraped across what is now the Ottawa Valley. Ten thousand years ago (give or take a millennium), as the ice finally retreated for good, it left behind the dramatic contours of a great rift valley between the Gatineau Hills and the long, granite fingers of the Canadian Shield. Rideau Hall is situated approximately 30 metres above the confluence of three rivers, a position that blesses it with a slightly warmer microclimate than the surrounding area. And though the winter winds come howling down from the north, they bring with them deep, protective blankets of snow.

Two kinds of rock bear up the site: limestone (which makes the soil alkaline) and granite (which makes it more acidic). Over this bedrock the retreating glaciers deposited a mosaic of alluvial and fluvial soils, ranging from pure sand to sandy loam and dense blue clay and varying in depth from a few millimetres above bedrock to 2 metres along streambeds. This mix of soils, along with the superb drainage of the gently sloping hilltop site, would have supported a wide variety of plants even before the area was cleared. It was then, as it is now, an ideal place for the creation of a northern garden.

Northern gardening isn't easy: the weather is either too hot or too cold, the winters are too long, and the growing season is too short in most parts of the country. But it allows for a much wider range of plants than most people assume possible, especially in areas where deep snow creates a natural mulch in winter. In this sense the Rideau Hall garden has more in common with gardens in Calgary or Quebec City than it does with the European gardens on which it was originally modelled. But, like every garden, it is singular. Soil varies widely from region to region, even from street to street. Every good gardener knows the local hardiness zone, which sets the general limits of the growing season, yet every garden has its own observable microclimate, or even several microclimates. The Rideau Hall garden is a quintessentially northern garden, but it is also unique in its particular site.

Above: An early 1880s photograph of the Gatineau River and the distant Gatineau Hills evokes European notions of the Romantic and the Picturesque as surely as any painting by Claude Lorraine. *Opposite*: Snow accents intact perennials and tree branches and appears to have added a hat to the sculpture of a Thai monk on the upper terrace. (The monk follows Clarkson and Saul from garden to garden like a talisman.)

The Grounds of Canada's House Today

1. Main Gate
   (1 Sussex Drive)
2. Main Drive
   (laid out by Lord Monck)
3. Parkland Area
4. Sugar Bush
5. Trillium Beds
6. Rideau Hall
7. Ambassadors' Court
8. Skating Rink
9. Conservatory
10. Greenhouses
11. Vegetable Garden
12. Herb Garden
13. Nuttery
14. Rideau Cottage
15. Lower Terrace
16. Perennial Borders
17. Connaught Dry Wall
18. Lady Byng Rockery
19. Norah Michener Rockery
20. Upper Terrace
21. New Perennial Garden
22. Tented Area
23. New Woodland Garden
24. Tennis Courts
25. Orchard and Vines
26. Canadian Heritage Garden
27. Thomas Gate
28. Visitor Centre
29. State Guesthouse
    (7 Rideau Gate)
30. Prime Minister's Residence
    (24 Sussex Drive)

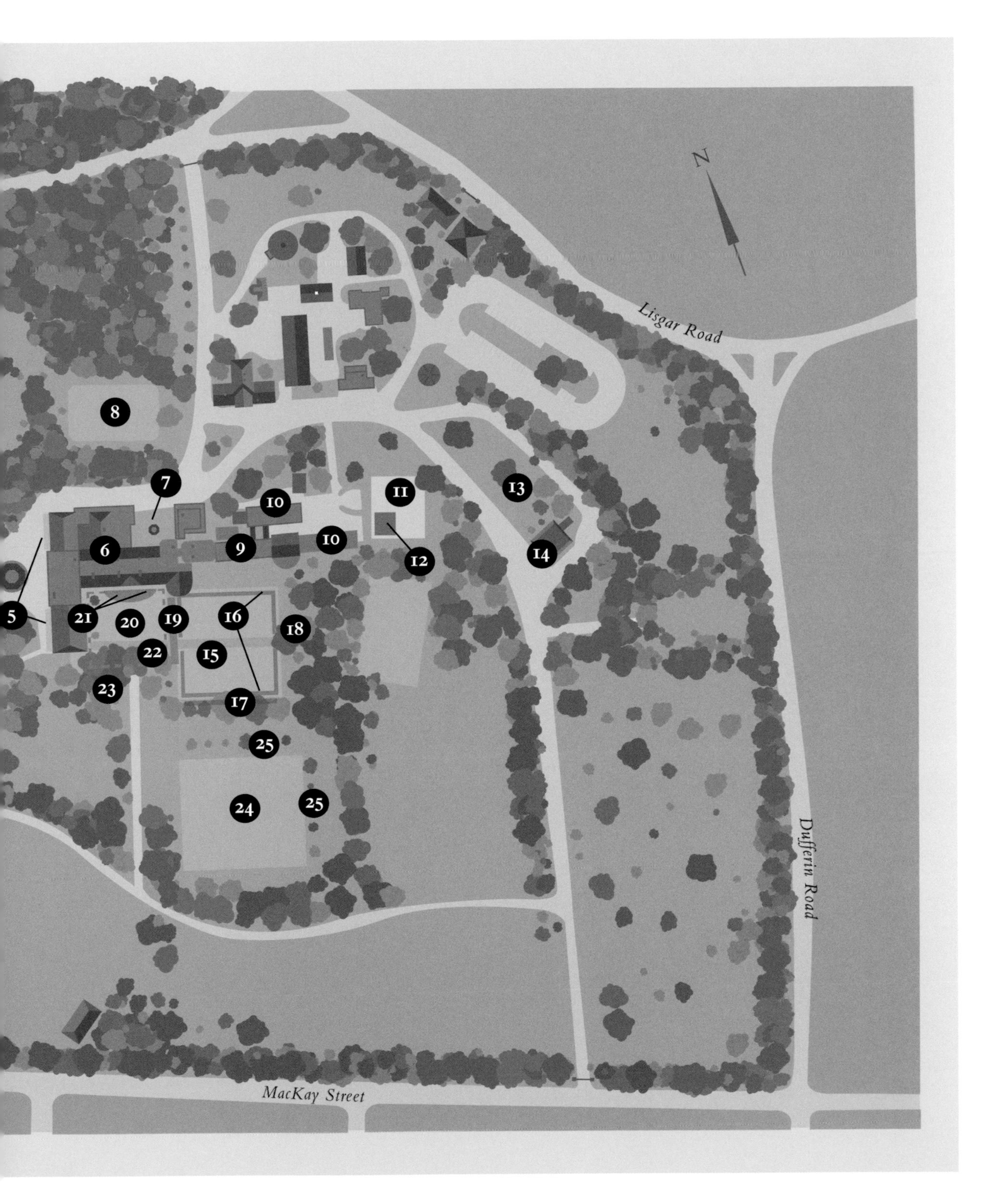
N
Lisgar Road
Dufferin Road
MacKay Street
5
6
7
8
9
10
10
11
12
13
14
15
16
17
18
19
20
21
22
23
24
25
25

It's doubtful that Thomas MacKay cared much about the quality of the soil or the variations in local microclimates in 1838, when he bought the 450-hectare tract of land that included the future site of Rideau Hall. MacKay, a successful local businessman, chose the property because it wasn't far from the grist and saw mills he operated on the Ottawa River (on land now in the Ottawa suburb of New Edinburgh). He cleared 40 hectares of his new property and set out to create an estate suited to his growing prosperity and social status. He built a house out of local limestone and placed it roughly in the centre of the cleared land on the highest spot in what is now Ottawa. Next to the house he planted a kitchen garden and laid out ornamental flower beds. To the southwest he established an orchard, while the area to the northeast became a working farm. When he was done, he had put in place all the essential elements of an English gentleman's country estate: parkland (the orchard and farmed land), ornamental gardens, a bowling green, a section of undisturbed forest suitable for rustic walks and woodland frolics, framed vistas of the magnificent surrounding countryside, and favourable views both from the house and of the house itself. MacKay managed the forested part of the property much as had the native people before him: he simply removed trees and underbrush to give the woods a more parklike feeling. The sinuous drive from Pine Street made a pleasant, though not very grand, approach to the front door.

Sunrise, by Claude Lorraine, is typical of the romanticized seventeenth-century depictions of nature that inspired the Picturesque tradition of landscape design, which in turn influenced the English Landscape style followed in the creation of the Rideau Hall estate.

After MacKay died in 1855, the house and grounds became available for rent. When, in 1864, the government of the newly created United Provinces of Canada started looking for a temporary residence for its first governor general, Rideau Hall seemed the obvious answer. Both the house and the grounds were small by English standards, but the location was spectacular and so, in 1865, the government leased the house and a portion of the grounds. Two years later Lord Monck, governor general of British North America since 1861, became the first governor general of the new Dominion of Canada. And, in 1868, Rideau Hall was purchased for $82,000, along with 35 hectares of land.

An 1882 wood engraving shows the Princess's Vista, which was created when Princess Louise ordered a section of woods to be cleared to provide a view from the house down to the Ottawa River. The vista filled in naturally over time. In recent years the National Capital Commission has thinned some of the trees so that the river is once again visible from the Rideau Hall property.

Even before Monck and his staff moved into Rideau Hall, however, he helped develop a plan to make it into a place worthy of his position as Canada's newly appointed head of state. This plan was a collaboration between three men: Lord Monck; Monck's chief gardener, Alpine Grant; and Frederick Preston Rubidge, the assistant chief engineer and architect of the newly formed Department of Public Works. All three carefully inspected the estate in 1864 and discussed possible changes before Rubidge began to draw up his initial plan later that year. The plan, along with the way Monck altered and embellished it, reflects the prevailing landscape aesthetic of the English Landscape style.

This style, much admired by the late nineteenth-century Canadian elite, called for rolling lawns, tree and shrub groupings, meandering paths, and woodland vistas. But Monck and Rubidge were also influenced (as Thomas MacKay had been) by the Picturesque style, which had been influenced, in turn, by the idealized seventeenth-century landscape paintings of Claude Lorraine, Nicolas Poussin, and Jean Antoine Watteau. The Picturesque emphasized the wildness of the landscape and strove to create a reality that emulated a painted scene, with ravines, waterfalls, and beautifully framed vistas. In Canada, of course, wildness was not hard to find. As one nineteenth-century commentator put it, "in spring, summer and autumn" Canadian country houses were surrounded "with scenery often denied to the turreted castle of the proudest nobleman in England."

In his 1865 plan, Rubidge stuck closely to MacKay's original layout, which had divided the estate into major zones. The area to the west of the main house was designated as well-wooded parkland; the area immediately to the south was to remain more open parkland (MacKay's orchard); and to the northeast, east, and southeast stretched arable land. (Budget constraints prevented Rubidge from removing "the unsightly Farm Buildings" to the northeast of the main house, but he managed to have a few of them torn down by 1878.) The parkland to the northwest, where MacKay had doffed his hat to the Picturesque, was kept intact—and eventually became known as the sugar bush. Finally, immediately adjacent to the south and east sides of the existing residence, Rubidge laid out ornamental gardens, private lawns, and a water feature (though it was never built). In the best English tradition, his initial budget set aside $140 to buy 400 trees with which to embower the house.

Monck and his wife, Elizabeth, moved into Rideau Hall in 1866 and immediately threw themselves into the garden project. In those days and for many years to come, custom dictated that the governor general pay for half the garden costs. Compared to a typical English country estate with many thousands of acres, Rideau Hall must have seemed very small indeed, but its gardens were still a major expense. For instance, it cost $800 a year to have almost 6,500 litres of soft water carted daily from the Ottawa River, until the Hall was connected with the city water mains in 1874.

Monck and his gardener Grant immediately began to implement much of Rubidge's plan, but they made one major change. Monck had never appreciated MacKay's modest tree-lined drive from Pine Street. He wanted a more impressive avenue to the house and decided on a lengthy sweep through the heavily wooded parkland to the west. In the best English Landscape style, this approach would conceal the house from visitors until it was suddenly revealed just before their carriage entered the circular drive to the front door. The wooded drive was also intended to create the illusion that the Rideau Hall estate was a much larger property than it actually was.

Another Monck innovation that survives today was a meandering gravelled walk through MacKay's forest to the north and northwest of the main house, making it a place where ladies could amuse themselves with pastoral woodland strolls along meandering paths. He also installed a sheltering

Imagining the Canadian Garden

The definition of a Canadian garden is simple: it's a garden that is true to Canada. Before you can plant a Canadian garden, you need to look closely at where you are. First that means looking at the site. What are the peculiarities of the local climate, the prevailing winds, the extremes of heat and cold, the reliability of snow cover in the winter? How good or poor is the drainage? What's the soil like? Then you have to ask yourself, what already grows around here? Only then can you start to ponder how these things all fit together. If you are true to the place, then your garden will grow. Gardens are like people: if they become what they are meant to be, they will thrive.

A garden is also a place that carries meaning. For one thing, it is where human beings lay out their vision of nature, their relationship to the natural world. A garden can build a wall against nature or it can erase the boundaries and welcome in the wild. *JRS*

The drive laid out by Lord Monck in the 1860s still presents the visitor with a grand approach that gives the impression the house is far more secluded and the estate far larger than they really are.

belt of trees around the perimeter of the estate to conceal it from the already encroaching city of Ottawa—and it proved useful too for keeping cows out of the gardens.

A fascinating 1868 photograph shows the rudiments of Rubidge's original garden design already in place. Lady Monck and a few of her seven children are seated on the lower terrace, which is laid out with flower beds carved in fanciful designs. The upper terrace, reached by climbing humble cedar steps cut into the grass embankment, is almost bare. Clearly, Monck and his gardener had a considerable way to go to realize Rubidge's vision. Only the flower beds of the lower terrace echo what the designer had in mind. It looks almost rustic compared with the initial design.

By the time Viscount Monck left office at the end of 1868, he, Grant, and Rubidge had begun the transformation that would eventually change "MacKay's Castle," with its modest surroundings, into a compressed version of an English country estate—a Canadian microcosm of the English macrocosm, where the public was welcomed only on special occasions. Rideau Hall at the time of Canada's birth seemed grand yet intimate, a place suitable for ceremonial purposes but also very much a home for the viceregal family.

Many governors general since Monck have put a stamp on the garden, but few made lasting changes. Flower beds and borders came and went with the reigning fashions of the day, shrubs and ornamental trees were planted and eventually died or were removed, but the essential shape—the underlying structure—of the garden remained the same. The bones of the garden we see today were all in place by the beginning of the First World War, when the Duke and Duchess of Connaught built an attractive stone retaining wall at the edge of the existing ornamental gardens, defining their southern boundary and providing a dramatic transition from the lower terrace to the parkland. The wall has survived.

After the Connaughts left Canada in 1916, the next significant alteration to the garden resulted from a change to the house. In the 1920s the 42-metre-long vine-laden verandah along the south side of the building was removed, no doubt

Lady Monck poses with four of her children in this 1868 photograph that captures the state of the ornamental gardens a year after Confederation. The upper terrace appears to be nothing more than lawn, but the lower terrace already shows evidence of the Victorian fascination with bedding-out plants in fanciful designs. The long verandah that would be removed in the 1920s can be clearly seen in the background.

because it was in poor repair and too costly to restore. But the removal of the verandah destroyed a crucial element in the transition from house to garden—that moment when you pause to switch gears as you move between inside and outside. In 1949 the last of the British-born governors general, Viscount Alexander of Tunis, tried to give the terrace a sense of enclosure by introducing the white wooden balustrade we see today. But all other attempts to solve this transition—a small, enclosed porch, a rose garden surrounded by boxwood hedging, and massed plantings of evergreens around the foundations of the house—eventually vanished.

Above: A corner of the Lady Byng Rockery today, where a hidden pool nurtures flowering water plants. *Opposite*: The front page of the article in the November 1926 issue of *Canadian Homes and Gardens* that celebrated Evelyn Byng's rock garden and saluted her positive influence on Canadian gardening.

Until the arrival of the Canadian-born governors general, the only viceregal gardener to change the garden permanently and for the better was Evelyn Byng, wife of Lord Byng of Vimy (1921-26). By the time she arrived in Ottawa she was an accomplished gardener with plenty of experience on her own estates in England. First she introduced the long walkway that runs all the way through the two terraces, giving them a central, unifying axis, and then she installed the large beds around the perimeter, filling them with perennials. Her most important legacy, however, is the rock garden.

Lady Byng was a hands-on gardener, and her "little rock garden," as she called it, was the trend-setter of its time. In the 1920s rock gardening was just hitting its stride as a horticultural fad, but her version was on a scale seldom seen then and almost never today. She astutely set it at the far eastern end of the long central walkway. (The carved stone bench in the centre now provides a satisfying focal point.) She gathered her rocks from the nearby neighbourhood of Rockcliffe Park and, once they were installed, she planted among them so skilfully that, from May to autumn frost, something was always in bloom. "She planted all kinds of flowering plants from all corners of the globe, many of which she had collected for her gardens in England and in Canada," wrote Alice MacKay in the November 1926 issue of *Canadian Homes and Gardens*. "Then she added a plentiful selection of Canadian plants. In every individual case she studied the native soil and surroundings of her plants, and then she sought to reproduce the home as closely as possible."

Overleaf: The splendidly restored Lady Byng Rockery shows off its fine form under a blanket of snow. (The stone bench was added later.)

Lady Byng's rockery, at Rideau Hall, Ottawa, the wild-flower corner, with its Canadian Orchids in the foreground, thriving hardily far from their habitat

LADY BYNG'S *AU REVOIR* TO CANADIAN HORTICULTURE

The first chatelaine to develop the gardens of Rideau Hall, Her Excellency leaves a gracious memory of her sojourn in Canada

By ALICE MACKAY

PLANTS and shrubs from her English gardens, from Belgium, Italy and France, wild flowers from the woods in Canada, alpine plants from the Rocky Mountains—of these Her Excellency the Lady Byng of Vimy made her rock garden at Rideau Hall, Ottawa. This and the new Maple trees, the Roses and Iris and hundreds of gorgeous flowering plants that have transformed the park where Government House stands, the garden-loving First Lady of the Land leaves as a gracious memory of her sojourn in Canada. For visitors of many years' standing at Government House observe that Lady Byng made of the spacious acres on the edge of Rockliffe Park a lovely garden area, attractive beyond the dreams of all her predecessors.

Perhaps no corner of the great private park of her Canadian residence was so dear to Lady Byng as her rock garden. Had she not chosen even the individual rocks in her walks through Rockliffe Park (a park which does not belie its name)? Had she not transplanted and transplanted numberless varieties of plants, seeking for each position and surroundings close to its habitat? No small work, as many an experienced gardener who has wrestled with his rockery will tell you! But Lady Byng had the patience and persistence of the real gardener. In three years she accomplished what normally it would have taken five years to do, and her joy in it was not lessened by the fact that she would have only a short season to enjoy it before returning to her own English gardens.

Her Excellency's recipe for the making of a rock garden was sufficiently simple that it might be imitated by most garden lovers. She gathered her stones from the closest neighborhood, which happened to be Rockliffe Park. She planned her planting so that she would have bloom from May until Autumn frosts. She planted all kinds of flowering plants from all corners of the globe, many of which she had collected for her gardens in England and in Canada. Then she added a plentiful selection of Canadian plants. In every individual case she had studied the native soil and surroundings of her plants, and then she sought to reproduce the home as closely as possible. All were hardy, and most of them were perennials, so that the beauty of the rockery would continue from year to year.

Cloud-blue Delphiniums offset the perfect old rose of the *Daphne cneorum*. Incidentally the last is not common in Canada

See also page 100

An interesting group of Daphne Cneorum in the centre with Primulas on the extreme left, Pansies and Rock Iris in the foreground

The Lady Byng Rockery, as it is now formally called, is exceptional, but it is also an exception. She seems to have been the first gardener at Rideau Hall to pay more than passing attention to the particulars of the place, to its Canadian soil and Canadian climate. On her many transcontinental journeys with her husband she hopped off the train at every opportunity and trudged off in search of native ferns and orchids, many of which she brought back to Rideau Hall. She also brought plants from her gardens in England and had them tested for hardiness at the Dominion Experimental Farm, recently established to conduct research for the Department of Agriculture.

The final important and lasting change to the original design came during the term of the third Canadian-born governor general, Roland Michener. In 1967, soon after the Micheners arrived at Rideau Hall, his wife, Norah, oversaw the installation of a second rockery, this one designed to make a well-demarcated, more attractive transition from the upper to the lower terrace. Almost-secret waterfalls characterized this elegant garden, which was then filled with the massed plantings of evergreen shrubs so popular at the time. The evergreens soon swamped the rockery but they did not destroy its underlying soundness. Now these huge dusty shrubs have been chopped back, to give them new life in some places and to be removed in others, replaced by more interesting plants.

For the next thirty years the Rideau Hall garden mostly rested. There were few gardeners among subsequent governors general or their spouses, and none who took the avid interest of Lady Byng or Norah Michener or, more recently, Gerda Hnatyshyn, who opened the Canadian Heritage Garden in June 2000. (The garden was designed by Alvin Regehr of the Canadian Heritage Garden Foundation and the original roses were chosen by Claire Laberge of the Montreal Botanical Garden to reflect the history of Canada and the many different peoples that live here.) Many viceregal couples spent their time at Government House without leaving a gardening footprint. But outside Rideau Hall's ornate gates, Canada was changing—and so were its gardens.

Statuesque ornamental grasses such as *Miscanthus sinensis* 'Silberfeder,' recently planted in the magnificent rockery created by Norah Michener in 1967, have transformed the slope separating the upper and lower terraces.

Across the country, gardeners were paying increasing attention to the microclimates they found in their own gardens. They were taking account of how different a garden in Calgary was from one in Toronto; or how the climate of Vancouver nurtured very different plants from those in Ottawa or in Halifax. Gardening became a regional phenomenon and a much more sophisticated art form. This more contemporary approach to gardening was finally acknowledged at Rideau Hall with the arrival of Adrienne Clarkson and John Ralston Saul, in 1999. Clarkson and Saul were serious gardeners before they arrived, well acquainted with what was already happening around the country. They had visited and learned from many gardens, both public and private, from coast to coast, among them Bill Terry's rock-laden garden near Sechelt on British Columbia's Sunshine Coast; Assiniboine Park in Winnipeg, an extraordinary perennial garden where lilies grow over 2 metres tall in a bitterly cold Z4 climate. Rideau Hall presented them with a wonderful opportunity: to help bring one of the country's most important gardens into the twenty-first century.

For many years, those dramatic flower beds in the lower terrace had been mainly replanted each year with masses of annuals for instant late spring and summer colour. In early spring the view of the lower terrace from the house was a sea of mud. On the upper terrace, only a small rose garden surrounding a stone reviewing pad used on ceremonial occasions relieved an area that was mostly stone and grass. The

Making Friends with Your Garden

Creating a garden is like starting a friendship. It takes time and effort and patience. A long friendship is the most demanding, important, and precious relationship you can have. I really believe that—and the older I get, the more I believe it. The best friendships are really a sort of extended conversation between equals. Even if your friend doesn't agree with you, or says things you don't like, or does something that drives you crazy, you keep talking to each other. You continue the conversation. Good friends don't try to change each other. It's similar with a garden. If you're not friends with your garden, it won't respond to you.

I've never met a serious gardener who didn't talk to her plants. But it's also important to talk to the site—especially when you are trying to envision a new garden. To create a good garden you have to listen to the place, start a conversation with it, find out what it's really supposed to be. The Rideau Hall gardens have been around an awfully long time, but they haven't always been listened to.

This is a big, inanimate place, crying out to be recognized for what it is—a repository of history, a place where people can come to experience their history in the present. It is a place where people are welcomed. So you must listen to your landscape and pay attention to what it is and what it wants. *AC*

What we learn from our surroundings when we watch and listen carefully and patiently is invaluable. I find that a solution to questions about how to deal with landscape . . . will gradually reveal itself.

FRANK CABOT

Ambassadors' Court, through which the prime minister passes each time he or she pays a call on the governor general, was a forgotten place. And the kitchen garden, once the gem of Rideau Hall, had pretty much disappeared.

Clarkson and Saul also brought with them a new gardening philosophy founded on three guiding principles: preservation, northernization, and Canadianization. These principles were formally adopted in a draft plan in 2000 by the National Capital Commission, which is responsible for both the house and grounds. They have now been enshrined in the National Capital Commission's long-term plan for maintaining and improving the Rideau Hall property—the Landscape and Site Management Guidelines of 2003. The principle of preservation rests on the goal of revealing the historical aspects of the garden that have been long neglected or have been gradually obscured. The site plan calls for preserving the hard landscape of the nineteenth century as well as highlighting the contributions of previous governors general, allowing for Rideau Hall's very Canadian interpretation of the British gardening tradition to become evident. The plan also permits the soft landscape to evolve naturally over time. The idea behind northernization is to emphasize native plants and hardy imported species that will flourish in the Ottawa climate, rather than fragile, exotic annuals from parts of the world with milder climates. And Canadianization simply means emphasizing "Canadian flora and cultivars." These days the Rideau Hall gardeners are encouraged to introduce plants native to Canada along with tough northern species from elsewhere. The underlying idea is to restore and maintain the best of the historic garden while enhancing it with the best of current Canadian gardening knowledge.

Of course, none of this could be done without the enthusiastic cooperation and hard work of the Rideau Hall gardening staff, all of them employees of the National Capital Commission. Fortunately, the team was incredibly skilled and highly knowledgeable about the unique attributes of this particular garden: Roeland Jansen, master

Rideau Hall's recent gardeners have been influenced by some of the finest contemporary gardens in Canada: Butchart Gardens near Victoria, BC (*opposite*); Kingsbrae Garden in St. Andrews, New Brunswick (*above*), with its handsome windmill; and Les Quatre Vents, the Quebec garden of Frank Cabot (*above right*).

JRS: "The best gardens are not created by committees but by a gardener (or a few gardeners) who has a strong idea of place. That's why the principles of preservation, northernization, and Canadianization are so important. That's why it's so important to adapt local, wild species into organized gardens."

arborist; Dagmar McCord, the expert on perennials; and Tim Welsh, who specializes in fruits and vegetables and now oversees the kitchen garden. They work under Mark Burleton, the manager of grounds and greenhouses, a highly experienced horticulturist and administrator.

This expert gardening team seized the opportunity to do something exciting and contemporary, something that would reflect the best Canadian gardening from coast to coast while always being true to the Rideau Hall site.

The Rideau Hall gardens were ripe for a revolution. But it has been a very Canadian revolution, one that has respected the past and learned from it. The result of these changes has much to teach us about gardens today but also about the value of historical models and the importance of patience. A garden is always a work in progress—and a garden created with a strong underlying vision can be altered and improved upon indefinitely, as long as you are true to that vision. Rideau Hall's first gardeners struggled against the site, striving to make an English garden where none could exist, but they didn't tamper with its underlying shape. We have learned from their example and can marvel at a garden that thrives in its northern climate and reflects in all sorts of ways the reality of the country.

Reflections on the Garden in Winter

There is nothing like a garden after the first real snow puts down that white blanket of eiderdown. I love the sense of lightness snow brings after the leaden days of late autumn when the trees are black and bare. Canadian gardeners always welcome the snow because it protects their plants from the coming deep freeze. And they know that a good snow cover will become nourishing meltwater that sinks into the earth next spring.

I love the way snow highlights the contours of a garden, revealing its underlying architecture. In a way, I suppose, looking at a garden in winter is a bit like looking at the face of a very old person whose skin has tightened to reveal the bone structure beneath. Of course, a hard winter or a winter without enough snow can be devastating to your garden. Since we've been at Rideau Hall, we've had rough winters where we've lost up to 20 percent of our perennials. So you have to be prepared to be disappointed. And you always have to be thinking ahead to next year. Which is one of the reasons serious gardeners spend a lot of time reading catalogues while their garden is covered in snow.

When you look at the Rideau Hall gardens in winter, you can see how sound their basic structure is. The original gardens were based on principles laid down in the late eighteenth century. As fads came and went, this underlying architecture became obscured. Some of the changes did fit the spirit of the place. Lady Byng's rock garden, for example—but even it had, at one point, almost completely disappeared under successive layers of soil.

Winter is a time of rest for the gardener, a time of reflection. It's a time to dream of colour and green. The garden in winter is a place for thinking about the fundamentals of your garden and for planning the future. *AC*

A photograph from a nearby roof reveals the elegant half-moon shape of the new perennial garden on the upper terrace.

CHAPTER 2

Spring Rideau Hall provides us with a model of how dynamic a Canadian garden can be in spring, and proves that many of our wild plants can flourish in domestic settings.

As part of the policy of Canadianization of the gardens at Rideau Hall, trilliums like these *T. grandiflorum* have replaced many of the exotic spring bulbs traditionally planted.

The New Woodland Garden

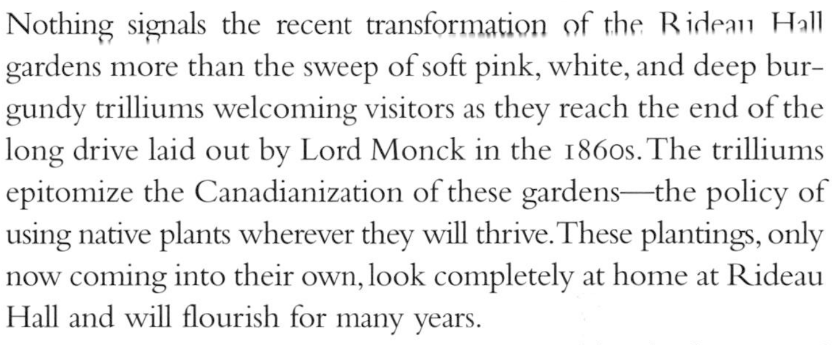

Nothing signals the recent transformation of the Rideau Hall gardens more than the sweep of soft pink, white, and deep burgundy trilliums welcoming visitors as they reach the end of the long drive laid out by Lord Monck in the 1860s. The trilliums epitomize the Canadianization of these gardens—the policy of using native plants wherever they will thrive. These plantings, only now coming into their own, look completely at home at Rideau Hall and will flourish for many years.

Until very recently, visitors were greeted by the legions of tulips planted every year. It was a tradition that began before the First World War, when Lady Grey began planting masses of these imported bulbs on the entrance grounds. To those who think of Ottawa as the tulip capital of Canada, the trilliums are unexpected, even startling, yet they are absolutely right for Canada's garden.

But the true star of the spring garden is the new woodland garden, which was developed by the gardeners, with the help of John Ralston Saul, to highlight the importance of cultivating native plants in an appropriate setting. It covers a narrow, gentle slope between the upper terrace and the lower playing field (where the annual staff picnic is held). A path lined by a wrought-iron fence covered with kiwi vines—they bear tiny fruit that never ripen—runs along the high side of this garden. Mature beech, maple, and oak trees create the graceful canopy needed for such a shade garden, while the path provides a splendid view of the whole.

The first woodland plants to appear in spring are known as ephemerals, so called because they last only until they are pollinated, and then retreat into dormancy until the following year. Most ephemerals bloom before the canopy leafs out. Other woodland plants require two essentials: high, dappled shade and humus-rich soil. While these cultural requirements (light and soil conditions) can be found in several places at Rideau Hall, the spot chosen for the woodland garden is ideal, close to a convenient strolling path often taken by visitors.

Saul had been inspired by visits to other contemporary gardens with woodland sections, above all Francis Cabot's "Les Quatre Vents" in Malbaie, Quebec, the most superb private garden in the country, and its woodland contains an extraordinary collection of native Canadian plants. These are gardens that have already demonstrated that Canadianization works in practice and that it can produce a brilliant contemporary garden.

The gardeners' first step was to take out the old plants and amend the existing soil. (The slope originally teemed with day lilies, spirea, and ferns, a strictly utilitarian means of keeping the bank from eroding.) They filled the beds with humus-rich soil and organic material similar to the duff found on a deciduous forest floor. Now they were ready to install the new woodland garden.

The main idea behind the design of this garden was to create a slice of Canadian woodland. Because of its placement—near to the more formal gardens of the upper and lower terraces—it would also make an attractive transition to the parklike area beyond. Where the paved walkway touches the woodland garden, a flagstone path meanders into the wood, creating the illusion that it is disappearing into the distance.

Saul and the gardeners marked out the edges of the planted section with yellow pencils to get an idea of the flow of the plants and how much space should be left for the pathway. Additional flagstones were placed off the garden path to allow the gardeners to work inside the bed without compacting the soil, something delicate woodland plants cannot tolerate. Finally, a huge boulder was set into the soil, but projecting a good metre above the surface, to provide a visual anchor at the beginning of the path. Here, as everywhere else on the site, the deployment of rocks and stones is inspired. The stones in the woodland border follow the direction of the glacial retreat. This clever touch of authenticity also gives the garden a more natural feel—as though the rocks and stones had been deposited by the retreating ice rather than painstakingly set in place.

Above: John Ralston Saul inspects the new woodland garden with Roeland Jansen and (almost completely hidden) Mark Burleton. In the foreground are hellebores, astilbes, and irises. *Opposite*: The woodland garden's flagstone path meanders through a mix of native plants and shade-tolerant perennials, including many types of ferns. To the left of the path are Japanese golden grass (*Hakonechloa macra* 'Aureola') and hellebores. On the right of the path in the foreground are wild ginger (*Asarum canadense*) and a form of bleeding heart (*Dicentra* 'Stuart Boothman'). In the background to the left of the path are the white plumes of false spirea (*Sorbaria sorbifolia*).

While the garden was being laid out and the soil enriched, Saul and the gardeners developed a garden plan adapted to the site and prepared a carefully researched plant list based on the conditions of low light and organic-rich soil. The National Capital Commission's Mark Burleton, who trained at the Royal Botanical Garden in Edinburgh, is now responsible for managing the grounds and greenhouses at Rideau Hall, as well as at the governor general's other official residence, the Citadelle in Quebec City. He takes a particular pride in the woodland—his favourite style of gardening. "The woodland garden is a combination of Canadian native plants and other northern-climate woodland plants," he says. "We are

The Essential Canadian Garden

A woodland or "wild" garden is the essential Canadian garden. Canada is a northern country, vast stretches of which are covered with forest. Even in our biggest cities the woods are not far away. And the most Canadian of gardens is a garden that welcomes native plants, either those that still flourish in the wild or those that were once native wild species. In Ottawa and most of the eastern part of Canada, that means a woodland garden. A woodland garden is one of the most beautiful and one of the easiest gardens to create—as long as you have a shaded area that mimics the conditions of a deciduous Canadian woodland. Such a garden acknowledges the reality of the northern country we live in.

Philosophically speaking, a woodland garden brings what I call "the territories" into our more settled places, whether cities or suburbs or rural areas. By the territories I mean that vast, sparsely populated northern upstairs that is so central to our national psyche, even if relatively few of us have ever been there. A woodland garden is about letting the rest of the country in. *JRS*

A spring carpet of colour in the new woodland garden mixes trilliums (*T. grandiflorum*), bleeding hearts (*Dicentra spectabilis*), and Virginia bluebells (*Mertensia virginica*), a native woodland plant.

trying to create a naturalistic planting, which will develop to provide interest for each season in this area. We have also grown some of the plants from seed for this garden—the seed we received from other well-known gardens. We did this because some species are hard to find in the nurseries." Some of these seeds came from the Royal Horticultural Society's Wisley garden in Surrey, England, where Burleton worked before coming to Rideau Hall; others came from botanical gardens in other parts of the country, as well as from plantspeople who specialize in growing from seed.

Whether the plants are natives or carefully selected non-native species, the goal was to come up with a mix that would grow well together and look natural in a Canadian setting. To this end, the gardeners layered the plants so that something would always be in bloom as the growing season progressed. The most difficult challenge was finding plants that grew naturally together and looked right. One approach that worked to create harmonious combinations was to select plants from the same family or in the same foliage and bloom tones.

At the top of this list were plants, such as trout lilies and bloodroot, already growing elsewhere on the Rideau Hall property. These ephemerals are among the first plants to pop up in the spring; then other early bloomers were added, including snowdrops (*Galanthus* spp) and liverwort (*Hepatica* spp). Then came the snouts of Solomon's seal (*Polygonatum biflorum*) and the emerging ferns. Trilliums are a major force in this woodland garden too. Planting successful swathes of them the first year encouraged planting of even more species in the second. Since it takes five years to grow a trillium from seed,

Three native plants in the woodland garden (*left to right*): Jack-in-the-pulpit (*Arisaema triphyllum*), lady slipper orchid (*Cypripedium acaule*), and yellow trillium (*T. luteum*). It's important to replicate the natural habitat of each native for it to thrive in a garden setting.

the gardeners were delighted to find a supplier who could provide mature plants of several species in large enough numbers to make a decent show by the second year. So far, four of the potential six trillium species have been planted—*T. grandiflora* (white), *T. erectum* (red), *T. undulatum* (painted trillium), and *T. sessile* (yellow trillium). The trilliums, which make a spectacular display lasting for weeks from early to late spring, will continue to multiply for decades to come.

In the first year, Burleton and his team brought in a great many primulas, but these plants didn't create the natural woodland look they wanted. They have since been supplemented with other shade perennials. The gardeners searched for ground covers no more than 15 centimetres high, such as wild ginger (*Asarum canadense*) and false lily-of-the-valley (*Maiamanthemum*), both native plants, along with lower-growing heucheras and masses of tiarella. Accompanying them there is Solomon's seal (*Polygonatum biflorum*), with *Rodgersia* spp to form upright contrasts. Two excellent autumn plants, both of Japanese origin, yellow wax bells (*Kirengeshoma palmata*) and various forms of the orchid-like toad lily (*Tricyrtis* spp), have such attractive clumping forms that they look right at home with the North American native plants.

Developing a rich woodland tapestry requires time. It takes several years to build up the right repertoire of plants, and at least two to three years for each round of planting to mature. That Rideau Hall's new woodland garden was completely planted within two years is a remarkable accomplishment—and it was done within the annual plant budget set by the National Capital Commission.

Wild Ginger

I wonder how many Canadians know that many of our eastern woodlands are full of wild ginger (*Asarum canadense*), a wonderful ginger that hasn't been genetically altered. You can start to harvest it even before the snow has melted because it comes up underneath the snow. It's proof that spring is coming. You can easily grow it in your backyard; in fact, it's now one of the underplantings in Rideau Hall's woodland garden. The chefs here use it to make wild ginger chocolates, and they put wild ginger in various desserts. When someone remarks on how delicious one of these desserts is, we tell them it's because of the Canadian ginger.

Wild ginger has a very Canadian character. It is somewhat secretive—its flower is hidden underneath the leaf—yet the flower is a very dramatic, dark purple. Isn't that how we imagine ourselves? We're colourful, but we're not sure about showing all our colours. Our qualities are partially hidden, but we're beautiful. And we're useful. *JRS*

As the woodland canopy leafs in, the colourful early spring ephemerals give way to the subtler tones of foliage, here a combination of variegated Jacob's ladder (*Polemonium caeruleum* 'Brise d'Anjou') in the foreground, Solomon's seal (*Polygonatum biflorum*) in the mid-ground, and the charming blooms of lungwort (*Pulmonaria*) in the background.

Above: One of the Rideau Hall summer apprentices, Leigh Derraugh, at work. *Opposite*: Woodland phlox (*Phlox divaricata*), a spreading, stem-rooting perennial that can slowly build a fairly large stand and gives a brilliant flash of spring blue to the woodland garden.

Recreating the Perennial Beds

The thinking at Rideau Hall during this period of northernization is to always start off with the right plant in the right place, fully satisfying its cultural demands of light and soil, and to mix perennials, shrubs, and trees in a way appropriate to the scale of the garden. In the old days in late spring, as soon as the ground was warmed up and the soil workable, the flower beds were planted with thousands of annuals. It was a philosophy of colour regardless of cost, colour beyond anything occurring in nature. The rule now is to have permanent plantings of perennials, with an emphasis on native plants supplemented by hardy annuals that harmonize with them.

Every flower bed on the estate starts off with good soil. This is partly a result of nineteenth-century construction methods. There were no landfills in those days, and the easiest place to toss rubble was in the backyard. As a consequence, all around the Hall there's plenty of coarse material beneath the topsoil, making for great drainage—one of the fundamentals of good growing. You never see puddles of water lying about, a sure sign the drainage needs attention. After decades of regularly adding topsoil to the beds, today's soil is deep and friable, or easily worked. Enhanced with manure, it will grow just about anything that can survive in the Ottawa climate.

The Rideau Hall gardeners use only natural fertilizers, now exclusively sheep manure, which has a much higher level of potassium and phosphate than cow manure and about the same level of nitrogen. The gardeners watch the manure like hawks to make sure it's well composted and that weeds aren't lurking about. The huge piles of leaves collected each fall and every bit of garden waste, except for diseased material, is composted. Even so, there never seems to be enough.

Getting to know the condition of a garden's soil is crucial because the soil indicates what kinds of plants will do well. It saves time and money in the long run. At Rideau Hall, organic supplements are added only if necessary. Usually the gardeners can tell by eye what's needed. Occasionally they mix soils from different parts of a bed and have it analyzed at the

During his tenure of office Lord Lisgar had cultivated the vegetable garden here at his own expense . . . But this year he will have left before any thing can come out of the garden, that is to say he would have to pay for sowing the seed while his successor would reap the fruits.

GOVERNMENT MEMORANDUM, 1872

Spring blooms in the Lady Byng Rockery include the pasque flower (*Anemone pulsatilla*) and these enchanting little irises (*I. cristata*).

laboratory of the Department of Agriculture to see what needs amending (any certified garden centre or agricultural school will do this inspection). In some instances, getting the soil right can be quite tricky. The native sandy loam (occasionally mixed with clay) is on the alkaline side, ranging from 6.9 to 7.6 on the pH scale (the higher the pH, the more alkaline the soil). But alkaline soil also ties up iron, which means that pin oaks and other plants needing a lot of iron will suffer chlorosis. A pin oak may start off with lovely green foliage in spring, but by summer the leaves have turned yellow. Once water-soluble iron is applied, however, the leaves turn green again in a day or two.

The raw materials at Rideau Hall are excellent. Good soil, good drainage, lots of light—the best of all growing circumstances. The results can be seen in the splendid mixed beds of perennials and annuals, of flowering plants and grasses and shrubs, that are already beginning to bloom in late spring, and in the herb and vegetable gardens.

The Potager

The Rideau Hall vegetable garden reinvents a long and honourable tradition that dates back to Thomas MacKay's time. The potager, or kitchen garden, has had a checkered history since then, although it lasted well into the twentieth century. It was converted to a tree nursery in 1956, but by the 1980s most of the trees had disappeared and it reverted to weeds and scrub. Today its enclosing hedge has been restored and a nuttery with species of edible nuts has been established immediately beyond. The overall effect is of a cloistered green sanctuary close to the house.

In the old days, the potager provided a substantial portion of the vegetables and all the herbs needed by the Government House kitchen. This tradition has been restored so that, these days, what's planted depends very much on what the chefs need. And every morning, from late spring until late fall, it is common to see several cooks in their white uniforms harvesting herbs and vegetables for that day's menu.

The potager itself is immediately adjacent to the greenhouse attached to the easternmost end of the house and covers an area 50 metres by 100 metres, surrounded by a hedge almost 3 metres high. Each of the eight vegetable beds is just over 90 metres square, with four beds on either side of a central pathway. They are irrigated by soaker hoses, which run down the rows and are operated by a timer. A border runs all around the interior perimeter of the garden, and a central herb garden occupies another 90-square-metre area just inside the entry gates. A low-strung electric wire surrounds the garden and proves to be an effective way to discourage groundhogs, rabbits, skunks, and squirrels.

For gardener Tim Welsh, spring comes in late winter to the greenhouses, where he starts vegetables that need longer than one hundred days to mature, as well as cold-tolerant early vegetables such as peas, radishes, spinach, leeks, potatoes, and chard, along with beets, carrots, and leaf lettuce. Greenhouse staff sow these vegetables in trays and pots, then harden off the seedlings in cold frames. By April at the earliest, they can plant the seedlings in the garden under the protection of hoop houses, or plastic tents. These tents automatically heat up even in the watery spring sunshine, causing extremely rapid growth for the plants inside. Once the frost has completely left the soil, usually by the end of May, any fairly well-developed seedlings are transplanted from the greenhouse straight into the garden without extra protection. A final planting of seeds grows on in the hoop houses until these shelters are removed in June.

This form of succession planting ensures that from early May to late November there will be fresh vegetables on the table. Because the intensive cultivation used in the hoop houses scoops all the nutrients out of the soil, they are relocated every year and the soil under them is replenished with plenty of manure. As everywhere on the Rideau Hall estate, the maintenance of the vegetable garden is completely organic and in step with the philosophy practised in the kitchens. No chemical fertilizers, pesticides, or herbicides are ever used. Beyond the well-composted sheep manure, very little fertilizer is even required.

This system reflects the growing interest in organic gardening in Canada. As people become more sensitive to the whole-

Above: Wooden boxes such as this one are useful to contain rapidly spreading plants such as mint. *Opposite*: Some lettuce seedlings are getting a good month's head start on the growing season in one of the plastic hoop houses.

Organic Common Sense

The vegetable garden at Rideau Hall has developed into something of a demonstration garden—a demonstration of what you can do when you respect the site and acknowledge the local climate. And that automatically means a garden that uses no chemical fertilizers or pesticides or herbicides—namely, an organic garden. A lot of people seem to have the impression that organic gardening is some kind of funny, funky thing where you grow spotty fruits and tiny vegetables. Then they take a tour of the kitchen garden here and they ask, "Why does everything look so healthy and big?" The answer is that these things belong here.

When you use chemicals, it becomes possible to pretend that you're somewhere else. But, ironically, the more naturally you grow things, and the more attuned to the place you become, the more your horizons expand. The growing season starts to get longer and it seems less artificial. The cooks here are now harvesting as early as the first week in May (for example, the gardeners start the lettuce under plastic tents as soon as the snow melts) until well after the first frost, right through to the middle of November. Certain vegetables love a touch of frost, like Brussels sprouts and butternut squash. It actually makes them taste sweeter.

You'd be amazed at how much of the food we serve to Rideau Hall guests comes out of the kitchen garden. It's because the gardeners haven't pretended that they're someplace else. They've worked with the site and embraced the fact that we live in a northern country. *JRS*

sale scattering of chemicals over their food supply, they tend towards the simpler and more sensible solutions presented by using organic methods. The Canadian Organic Growers, a group that used to appeal only to organic farmers, is steadily growing in popularity. Nowadays it's attracting more and more home gardeners as it becomes increasingly influential. Organic gardeners are being increasingly seen as worthy stewards of the environment, practitioners of good old common sense.

The perennial challenge of the organic vegetable garden is pest control. Tim Welsh has tried various techniques, notably companion planting. This approach involves planting a species that will trap or repel an insect next to a vegetable on which the pest likes to feed. For instance, marigolds planted among tomato plants are reasonably effective at keeping away nematodes. Another trick is interplanting tomatoes with other vegetables. "The bugs then have a hard time finding what they're looking for," Welsh says, "but they would zone in on a whole bed of tomatoes on their own." Basil repels tomato worms and also acts as a trap plant. Nasturtiums, which are a magnet for aphids, are also good to eat.

The herb garden is based on a traditional checkerboard style that goes back to medieval times. It consists of a pattern of alternating squares of stone and squares of soil. The garden is fifteen squares by fifteen, or 225 squares in all. The stones allow easy access to any part of the bed, while keeping each herb separate, and they also cut down on weeding.

Opposite top: The checkerboard herb garden contains more than enough unusual and obscure herbs to continually challenge the Rideau Hall kitchen staff. *Opposite below:* Executive chef Oliver Bartsch and executive sous-chef Louis Charest picking what's ready for the table as they plan that day's menu.

The garden in spring is a garden in transition, from one season to the next. Its brief moment of glory comes with the blooming of the ephemerals and other springtime natives, especially the wonderful display of trilliums. As summer approaches with its dense canopy of leaves, more subtle woodland plants like ferns, dead nettle (*Lamium* spp), and false spirea (*Astilbe* spp) take centre stage. No visitor to Rideau Hall in spring would mistake these gardens for anything but Canadian. They show us what is possible in almost any region of the country. Depending on local conditions, the mix of native and non-native plants will vary, but the overall result can be elegant and enduring. Rideau Hall provides us with a model of how dynamic a Canadian garden can be in spring, and proves that many of our wild plants can flourish in domestic settings, looking right at home.

How lovely it was then to see the sheets of blue, yellow and white violets, the swaying beauty of lemon-coloured bellworts, the coarse-foliaged arbutus hiding its fragrant shell-pink blossoms in loamy woodlands.

EVELYN BYNG

White peonies, part of Rideau Hall's superb peony collection, dominate this view from one of the perimeter beds on the upper terrace. The peonies play nicely with the pink-and-white irises beyond them and their foliage contrasts nicely with the nearby lady's mantle (*Alchemilla mollis*), with the blue wings of Siberian iris (*I. sibirica*), and with the bleeding heart (*Dicentra*). (A large single white peony was named for Adrienne Clarkson in June 2004 by the Canadian Peony Society.) Beyond the balustrade stretch the colourful perennial beds of the lower terrace.

CHAPTER 3

Summer Sitting in the middle of this garden on a summer day means being surrounded by colour and scent, a heady experience almost like sitting in the middle of a meadow.

One dense corner of the lower terrace perennial garden: purple garden phlox (*Phlox paniculata*), yellow *Rudbeckia hirta*, white Japanese anemone (*Anemone japonica*), and, in the immediate foreground, *Gaura lindheimeri*.

A Garden for Canadians

Most days throughout the year the grounds of Rideau Hall are now open to visitors from 8 a.m. to sunset, but in late June, the governor general also throws the annual garden party and invites Canada in. They come by the thousands: people from Ottawa and from other parts of the country, and tourists from around the world visiting the nation's capital. They wander about the grounds, sip iced tea, and nibble on cookies. But it's the gardens that most of the visitors have come to see—now at their brilliant best.

And what a sight they are: breathtaking waves of colour, one shade drifting subtly into the next; an eye-popping mix of perennials and grasses, trees and shrubs, and a few carefully chosen annuals that float among the perennials, knitting them together in singular combinations; a kitchen garden already ripe with early summer vegetables; and a herb garden with more unusual species than most of us have heard of. In the impressive flower gardens of the upper and lower terraces, many of the plants are labelled for the benefit of interested visitors, but not so obviously as to give the feeling of a botanical garden, and people are more than likely to be seen making notes on discoveries about plants native to the area or new plants from many other parts of the country and from other northern parts of the world. In one of the rock gardens they can even admire a few tundra plants recently brought back from the Yukon, among them the dwarf rhododendron.

Given the nature of the Canadian climate—extreme cold alternating with extreme heat—planting large and graceful borders that work as well as they do at Rideau Hall is no easy task, and not just because of their huge scale. Contemporary gardening wisdom holds that biodiversity and variety are the basic elements of the well-built garden bed, and these two principles are in evidence throughout the gardens today. And we can see how even the most formal and public of Canadian gardens can reflect our climate and express the nature of our place.

Recreating the Upper Terrace

In 1999 the most immediate problem area in the existing gardens was the upper terrace, an area that had baffled successive tenants since the removal of the long verandah in the 1920s. The difficulty was twofold: the abrupt transition from house to garden and the impersonal feel of the terrace itself, the only outdoor space on the grounds reserved primarily for the governor general's personal use. It is roughly the size of an average suburban garden. It also serves as the central gathering place for lawn parties and after medal ceremonies.

In 1999 the upper terrace was still dominated by three large rectangular cement pads. The one closer to the house was mostly used as a reviewing stand on ceremonial occasions

Above: In late summer the new perennial garden appears to flow out from the side door onto the upper terrace in a colourful stream that includes asters (*Aster* 'Harrington Pink'), lavender, and penstemon. *Opposite*: In this 1904 photograph, the upper terrace is framed by the wing that houses the indoor tennis court.

and, occasionally, as a patio. The one beyond the central walkway that runs the length of the upper and lower terrace was covered with an open-sided tent and used for serving meals. The lawn surrounding these paved areas was not conducive to strolling because there was nowhere to stroll to, and the small boxwood hedge that encased the reviewing pad tended to be intimidating. The total effect was stiff and uncomfortable. In winter, especially, the view from the sunroom, where breakfast and lunch are often served, was downright dispiriting.

The whole area needed to be warmed up and visually knit together. Like previous governors general, Clarkson brought with her memories of public and private gardens visited across the country. These included the Butchart Gardens near Victoria, British Columbia, the University of British Columbia's Asian Garden (with its impressive pathways), the heritage perennial garden on the Seager Wheeler Farm near Rosthern, Saskatchewan, the Toronto Music Garden, the Montreal Botanical Garden, Kingsbrae Garden in St. Andrews, New Brunswick, and Halifax's Public Gardens (recently devastated by a hurricane).

As a first step, she and the Rideau Hall gardeners decided to remove most of the cement reviewing pad next to the house, along with all the boxwood hedge, the spireas, and any other tired plantings. They saved the species roses (*Rosa rugosa*) and, because of their scent and their huge rosehips, transplanted them closer to the house. That left a yawning triangle of exposed soil in the middle of the lawn: at this point, the upper terrace was a tabula rasa.

Over the following winter Clarkson and the garden team looked at this empty space and thought about the problems—for instance, how to deal with the relentless sun—and the potential for exciting colours and plant combinations that would help bring new life to this historic area. What emerged the following spring was a comprehensive plan, the centrepiece of which would be a very large, colour-drenched, intensely planted perennial garden tucked right up against the house and projecting into the lawn in a half-moon shape. They chose this configuration to break up the formality of the terrace and soften the transition from the house to the garden.

Above: Adrienne Clarkson with gardeners Dagmar McCord (*standing*) and Tim Welsh in the new perennial garden, with a cheerful swath of luminous salmon-pink poppies (*Papaver orientalis* 'Helen Elizabeth') in the foreground. *Opposite*: This view of the new perennial garden shows the way its half-moon shape seems almost an extension of the house. The stone path and central patio make it into an inviting garden room.

The overall plan included deep borders next to the house and around the perimeter of the terrace. The tent pad on the side away from the house would be retained, and the more shaded bed next to it expanded to become a natural green wall along one side of the covered dining area all summer long.

Dagmar McCord, the perennials expert on the garden team, worked with Clarkson to lay out the new bed. One morning early that spring McCord could be seen crawling along on her hands and knees adjusting a garden hose while Clarkson moved from second-floor window to window above, calling out suggestions, which were supplemented by comments from anyone who happened to be passing by. McCord pushed and pulled the hose until it outlined a garden that seemed to them both to be the right scale. A good old hose will work to outline the shape of a new bed anywhere, it seems.

This dramatic new flowerbed, with well-drained, deep, and rich soil, was immediately ready for planting. Because it faces south and receives the full intensity of the summer sun as well as heat radiating off the house, the gardeners knew they had to choose plants to withstand this withering exposure—hardy perennials, sun-loving annuals, and ornamental grasses. In addition, Clarkson wanted to harmonize the colours of the terrace garden with those of the adjacent rooms inside the house, to enhance the illusion in summer that the terrace is an extension of the house. To achieve this effect, she chose a simple palette in which salmon, pink, and purple predominate, and with blues, mauves, and whites used as contrast. Plants such as lavender, magenta yarrow (*Achillea millefolium*), and rich pink carnations (*Dianthus deltoides*) became this garden's perennial backbone. Other tried-and-true perennials added to the mix included hardy geraniums like *G.* 'Johnson's Blue' and white and pink mallows (*Lavatera* spp).

All these perennials were supplemented with other sturdy reliables such as *Gaura lindheimeri*, which in its native Texas is a perennial but in most parts of Canada must be treated as a self-seeding annual. Gaura reaches the useful height of about one metre, and produces white-to-pink flowers at the end of

Colours and Combinations

A mistake people often make when planning their garden is to think of it as primarily a decorative task. If you set out to decorate your backyard the way you might decorate your living room or your den, then you're in for trouble. I'd say the two most important criteria in creating a successful garden are variety and chronology. By variety, I mean a diversity of species: within reason, the more different plants, the merrier. By chronology, I mean knowing when different species are going to bloom.

The best perennial garden is one that blooms steadily from late spring until early fall, one where there's something new happening every week or two. That's what my mother's garden was like. There was always lots of colour. Tulips in May, peonies in June, followed by delphiniums and baby's breath. In July I particularly remember her Asiatic lilies, and in August her dahlias and gladioli (two tastes I didn't inherit). So you want things to be flowering right through. And you want a variety of species and a number of different colours that complement each other. *AC*

long, wiry stems for a cheerful, sprongy effect, especially when the blossoms dance like butterflies in a gentle breeze. Later that spring the gardeners planted summer bulbs, including peacock orchid (*Acidanthera bicolor*), which has a pure white blossom with a blue-purple eye—a colour flawlessly picked up in the purple of a nearby hardy geranium.

So far so good. But it seems like an unwritten gardening rule that no matter how big you make a border, once you've seen it in flower, you'll want it even bigger. And sure enough, when the half-moon bed came into full bloom, it was immediately apparent that it should be expanded the following spring. The gardeners selected additional plants specifically to pick up the original tones. They included a velvety deep magenta *Penstemon* 'Husker's Red', which bumped up the pinks of the mallows, and an apricot mullein, *Verbascum* 'Helen Johnston', to contrast with the penstemon.

A good principle in choosing any garden palette is to keep it simple. Three or four shades, with one tone shifting into another, creates an amazingly satisfying overall effect. The crowning touch in this expanded garden bed was another of Clarkson's ideas: to make a pathway of elegant rectangular stepping stones running from the house towards the stone patio (a remnant of one of the original stone pads) in the centre part of this now-enlarged bed. Sometimes chairs are put out on this patio; at other times it is a popular spot for informal photographs of visitors. Sitting in the middle of this garden on a summer day means being surrounded by colour and scent (the plants were also chosen for their fragrance), a heady experience almost like sitting in the middle of a meadow.

On the steps of the glassed-in Verandah are large pots of *Agapanthus*, or lily of the Nile. In the background echinacea and *Lychnis coronaria* accent the sweep of summer colour in the half-moon perennial border.

But the rest of the upper terrace—where, as you move towards the tented area, the light softens from full sun into dappled shade—also needed some attention. The small beds next to the house were widened, as were the beds along the other three sides of the terrace, and planted with large shrubs and new perennials. The borders around the perimeter of the house each have a special muted palette, in sharp contrast to the saturated colours of the half-moon garden. Along the eastern railing bordering the upper terrace, for example, the gardeners planted euphorbias and a variegated Jacob's ladder (*Polemonium* 'Brise d'Anjou'), whose mounded forms, combined with tall grasses, now frame the view of the lower terrace and provide a foretaste of the plantings beyond.

The technique of picking up a small tone from one planting and repeating it in a nearby one has been used throughout the garden, and it has proved especially effective in the cool oasis by the tent, shaded by a mature ash. Here Dagmar McCord has emphasized foliage rather than blooms, creating a restful Zenlike atmosphere where people pause to rest or eat.

There is already a mature and settled quality to the upper terrace, a coherent transition from the house to the garden, and the house itself is echoed in the gentle drifts of bloom ranging from pale salmon to burgundy and rich purple. The porch is still too small by comparison to the size of the house, but the eye is immediately drawn to the huge containers and lush plantings on either side of the steps leading from it and to the dramatic flower bed beyond.

Exterior Decorating

Deciding what you're going to plant where is when you get to be a bit of an exterior decorator—choosing flowers that fit your personal colour palette, work well together, and suit the shape and depth of your particular garden. Ordinarily I wouldn't plant anything that was bright yellow, such as evening primrose. The strong yellow tends to overwhelm the more subtle shades. But the Rideau Hall gardens are big enough and deep enough that, by planting yellow primroses off in the distance, you get a wonderful effect: they look like little lights against the green, especially at dusk.

I tend to favour softer shades: dark burgundy rather than bright red, peach rather than pink, mauve rather than purple, ochre rather than yellow. And then there are many shades of green, all sorts of wonderful perennial shrubs and grasses with many leaf shapes and textures. The trick is to imagine, to visualize what these combinations of colour and texture will look like at each phase of the blooming season. This is a contemplative activity that I particularly enjoy.

Even if your garden is small, you can think of it as a series of smaller outside rooms that are marked off in some way, not just by paths and borders or trees and hedges but by colour. It's amazing how much you can do with a very small city garden, as long as you respect the site. *AC*

A glorious summer moment in the Norah Michener Rockery demonstrates the effectiveness of subtle colour combinations. The purple of creeping phlox (*Phlox subulata*) along with an assortment of sedges contrasts splendidly with the graceful sprinkling of bright blue fescues and the golden false cypress (*Chamaecyparis pisifera*), as well as a variegated Japanese willow (*Salix integra* 'Hakuro Nishiki').

Three stalwarts of the summer garden (*left to right*): Biennial foxgloves (*Digitalis purpurea*), which set plants the first year and bloom the second; bearded iris, one of many iris species on display; and the elegant *Lilium canadensis*. The extraordinary repertoire of plants at Rideau Hall shows how vast a selection is available to northern gardeners.

A More Public Space

The walk down the eight steps from the upper to the lower terrace, past the Michener Rockery, is to travel from an intimate, almost private, space to a more public one. The lower terrace is the largest and most formidable ornamental garden at Rideau Hall, grand but not grandiose. Except for the central walkway introduced by Lady Byng in the 1920s, it has retained its overall design since the beginning of the twentieth century: a gigantic square of grass defined on all four sides by 3-metre-deep flower beds. Its size—over 800 square metres with approximately 450 square metres of beds—would be enough to intimidate most gardeners. As a result, many previous tenants left it to the gardeners of the day and the fashions of the moment, with orders simply to keep it filled and keep it bright.

Borders on this scale need to be designed with an almost painterly eye and a sense of all four seasons. And Clarkson brought both these qualities to bear. She envisioned dramatic plantings of ornamental grasses—massed colours rather than masses of plants, colours that echo in drifts. The skeleton within the borders—small trees, large shrubs, and woody plants—keeps the basic shape intact all year round. And within this structure the patterns of plantings will change year by year.

Each of the beds of the lower terrace is a case study in how to plant a sunny Canadian summer garden. Each employs a limited range of colours within considerable diversity of species. Each is defined by the towering ornamental grasses (miscanthus in a variety of species and named forms such as *M. floridulus* and *M. sinensis* 'Gracimillis'), which act like sentinels at either end. Take, for example, the southern border above the dry wall.

Here the gardeners preserved the glorious peony collection with its wide range of colours, which blooms magnificently in May and June along with the bachelor's buttons (*Centaurea* spp) and meadow rue (*Thalictrum*), two species that have been growing along this edge for almost a hundred years. But now these much-loved traditional flowers are contrasted with contemporary favourites: large alliums, with their big

Opposite: A view from the upper terrace over the lower terrace lawn and its 3-metre-deep perennial borders in early September.

Overleaf: A panoramic view of the lower terrace in late summer with the tented patio of the upper terrace in the background. In front of the tent (where many meals are eaten in warm weather) the white balustrade defines the division between the terrace and the Norah Michener Rockery. This is definitely a garden that makes the visitor feel comfortably cosseted by nature.

Above: A red opium poppy (*Papaver somniferum*), which waves like a crimson silk handkerchief in a gentle breeze. *Opposite*: A perennial border on the lower terrace at its early summer peak makes a picture-perfect combination. Blue delphiniums dominate the background, against which the red bee balm (*Monarda*), pink foxgloves, and the allium heads now gone to seed still look lovely. The cluster of greenish-white and pink blooms in the right background is masterwort (*Astrantia major*).

globelike white heads, and variegated Jacob's ladder. Throughout the border, masses of salvias and solid clumps of perennials – spikes of Siberian irises or groupings of martagon lilies, poppies such as *Papaver* 'Patty's Plum' or *Chrysanthemum* 'Clara Curtis', lupines (from Adrienne Clarkson's mother), and *Tradescantia* 'Concord Grape'—ensure that the garden will have colour from spring to fall.

Regardless of what's in flower, a glorious variety of perennial and annual grasses provides constant interest. As well as the imposing grasses at either end, they include Chinese fountain grass (*Pennisetum rubrum*) and prairie switch grass (*Panicum virgatum* 'Warrior'), whose feathery red flower heads are stunning when backlit by the sun. Everywhere the enchanting gaura and magenta cleomes have seeded themselves in absolutely the right spots. Punctuating this already intense variety are apple trees, including Northern Spy, Golden Russet, and Red McIntosh, each with a different clematis winding up its trunk.

What is dazzling about these borders is the sense of unity they convey from one section to the next while filling such a considerable space. Waves of colour pass from one tone into the next, until you hit a new hue that harmonizes with what's gone before and what comes after. It is a tapestry-like way to garden, and it has an obvious effect on visitors. You see them stop suddenly to gaze at a mingling of purples and pinks, before moving on to a green and white transition section or returning more than once to a blue and citron-yellow medley. The lower terrace has been transformed from what was once a stiff and uncomfortable hot spot into a place of great beauty and contemplative ease.

Lady Byng Uncovered

The changes on the lower terrace demonstrate a respect for the past combined with a very modern sensibility. This approach has been at work in the Lady Byng rockery, now liberated from a long period of neglect. Over the years it had become overgrown with yew and other evergreens and almost buried in successive layers of topsoil, as each year's bulb display was planted up. The rockery had gradually evolved into a great mound of soil with a few rocks jutting out.

Bringing this garden back began as a kind of archaeological dig, directed by Roeland Jansen. First he and his team got rid of just about everything growing in the mound except for some of Lady Byng's finds. The overgrown shrubs were whacked back almost to the ground. Even so, only a hint of the original rock garden was visible. But one by one enormous, magnificent rocks slowly emerged. "I said 'There's a rock! Uncover it,'" Jansen recalls with relish. "And it was beautiful, so I said, 'Okay guys, out with the soil and uncover another rock.'" As more and more rock became apparent, it was clear to him that they'd come from nearby. "If you go out on the point across from the prime minister's house," he says, "and you look at the formation of the rock over there, it is very similar to what we were exposing."

When Jansen and his team had completed their excavation, Lady Byng's original rockery had been brought back into the light. Only a few of the ferns and wild orchids she had gathered have survived, but the new plantings have remained true to her vision: a loose mix of native plants such as pasque flower (*Anemone pulsatilla*), along with pruned evergreens, cascade from the top of the rock formation to create a waterfall effect that doesn't swamp the beauty of the stones themselves—stones whose apt placement is once again readily apparent. And as a focal point at the end of the long walk, the rockery is a perfect foil to the formal terrace gardens, just as Lady Byng no doubt imagined it would be one day.

The summer gardens at Rideau Hall deftly show just what glory is possible in our northern climate. Throughout, there is a sense of rich botanical variety integrated into an aesthetic whole. The gardens also reveal the very best of contemporary thinking about garden design and plantings, while holding on to something that is important to us historically. This balance between past and present is as exquisite as it is rare.

Above: Behind the stone bench that acts as the focal point of the Lady Byng Rockery blooms an old standby, bridal wreath spirea (*Spiraea* 'Arguta'). Evergreens, like those in the foreground, are now kept well trimmed so they won't obscure the rocks beneath. *Opposite:* Red canna lilies, water iris (*I. versicolor*), and water lilies (*Nymphaea odorata*) are among the amazing variety of water plants that thrive in just one of the rockery's several secret pools, part of an elaborate water feature at the back of this historic garden. (The lettuce-like plant to the right of the iris is *Pistia stratiotes*; the corkscrew-shaped plant just beyond the water lilies in the foreground is *Juncus effusus spiralis*.)

Above: The Lady Byng Rockery in full summer bloom is animated by layer upon layer of plants: a swath of evergreens, purple Japanese irises and mauve alliums, white *Anemone canadensis* and puffs of *Anemone pulsatilla* that have gone to seed. *Opposite*: This iridescent Himalayan blue poppy (*Meconopsis betonicifolia*) was brought to Rideau Hall from British Columbia. AC: "Ever since I first saw a picture of a Himalayan blue poppy in *Taunton's Fine Gardening* magazine many years ago, it has struck me as an almost mystical plant. It grows in quite a few places in Canada, but I never thought I'd be able to grow one in any garden I had. I wasn't very hopeful when we planted a handful here at Rideau Hall. Then, bang, the following June we had four beautiful blue poppies. I consider it a major triumph. It was like a dream come true. In 2004, there were no blooms. My heart, though cracked, was not broken. Gardeners live on hope."

CHAPTER 4

Autumn To replace dying native trees is a particularly tricky process. Some of the maples on the grounds are well over a hundred years old and, when they die, they leave gaping holes.

Tagetes (a small marigold used as an insect deterrent) blooms beneath a row of sweet pepper plants, behind which are Brussels sprouts and tomatoes. The vines in the background bear table grapes.

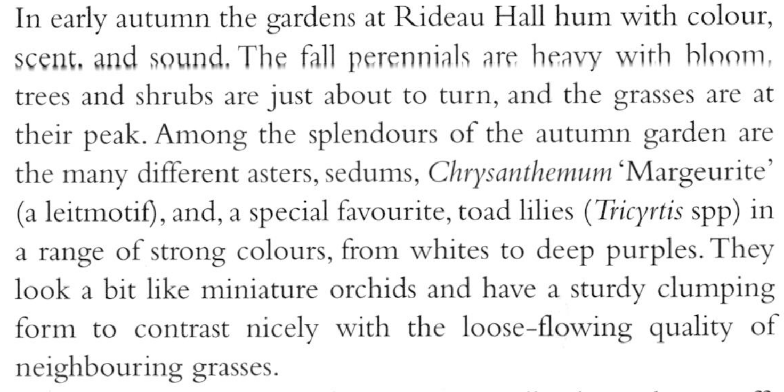

In early autumn the gardens at Rideau Hall hum with colour, scent, and sound. The fall perennials are heavy with bloom, trees and shrubs are just about to turn, and the grasses are at their peak. Among the splendours of the autumn garden are the many different asters, sedums, *Chrysanthemum* 'Margeurite' (a leitmotif), and, a special favourite, toad lilies (*Tricyrtis* spp) in a range of strong colours, from whites to deep purples. They look a bit like miniature orchids and have a sturdy clumping form to contrast nicely with the loose-flowing quality of neighbouring grasses.

All perennials take a few years to really show their stuff, and grasses are no exception. But most grasses will outlive flowering perennials and, once established, require very little care. Many are drought tolerant, and most need only to be cut back in spring and given the occasional feed of manure. At Rideau Hall they are divided every three or four years and distributed to other parts of the garden.

But autumn is not just about savouring the last of summer's beauty; it is also about rituals of passage, about preparations for winter and plans for spring. In the kitchen garden the herbs and late-harvest vegetables such as Brussels sprouts, winter kale, and butternut squash are still being harvested. When the harvest is complete, almost everything else is pulled out and thrown on the compost heap. What's left behind—the bamboo supports for beans, the ferny asparagus tops, the trees planted for temporary winter protection—keeps the potager attractive long after winter sets in.

Throughout the estate, the apprentices race to get the mountains of leaves gathered up before they must head back to school. They also help the full-time gardeners with selective planting of various bulbs, pruning hundreds of trees and shrubs, and establishing new ones while the soil is still warm and filled with oxygen. As the season progresses, vulnerable young trees and shrubs are wrapped in burlap. And, if there's time, the soil in the vegetable garden will be turned over, but no one fusses. It's one of those jobs that can wait until spring.

Opposite: A white aubergine (eggplant) ripens amidst *Tagetes* blossoms. *Above*: A view of the kitchen garden in early October, where a rich array of produce is still being harvested. Behind the Brussels sprouts are rows of purple kale, one of the hardiest leaf vegetables.

Autumn Beauty

In a Canadian garden you never simply plant for one season, you plan for the whole year. The way you experience a garden through its various seasons is a little like turning the pages of a good book. The trick is to make sure each page brings you something new. In a well-planned summer perennial garden something new will be in bloom about every two weeks. The hardest chapter of the book to write is Autumn.

Fall in the garden is the season of what Shakespeare called "the sere, the yellow leaf," when leaves turn to gold and brown. But there are also a number of plants that first flower in the fall or keep on flowering until the first frost and sometimes beyond. Chrysanthemums, particularly the daisy-like variety that range from a kind of ochre to a dusky rose, enhance the sense of fading beauty. One of my most successful recent autumn discoveries is the Formosan toad lily *(Tricyrtus)*, which has a wonderfully delicate-looking orchid-like flower. There are quite a few varieties: some are all white, some are white speckled with purply red. Formosan toad lilies start blooming in late August and they can sit there quite happily with the snow on them. We've had great luck with them here. Some of them grow to be more than a metre high.

Autumn is a golden time. And if you've planted your garden well, its colours and shapes and textures will continue to evolve well after you've turned the page to winter. *AC*

Just before the first hard frost, a generous layer of fresh mulch is spread around flowers, shrubs, and trees to help plants through the coming winter. In any northern garden, the best possible protection is a blanket of snow, but even in Ottawa, a city of deep snow, this cover can't always be counted on. Mulch is the cold-climate gardener's best possible trick to keep the plants safe.

In spite of a massive year-round composting campaign, there is never quite enough mulch to make the depth required for insulating the soil. So the gardeners supplement it with other organic material such as ground-up leaves and finely chopped cedar bark (when they run out of compost, the cedar bark is used by itself). This mulch not only provides effective protection for such a harsh site but gives the gardens an even, consistent look.

Covering perennial beds with mulch and piling it around the base of shrubs and trees without actually touching the stems or trunks (it causes rot) is one of those rituals that connect the gardener with the garden. A 10-centimetre-deep layer of mulch will keep soil temperatures even. During thaws, followed by another bout of freezing weather, the soil can expand and contract. This freeze-thaw reaction can pitch a plant right out of the ground.

Another important autumn task at Rideau Hall, one that continues through the winter and into early spring, is pruning hundreds of trees and shrubs throughout the estate. Tyros among the garden helpers get to hone their pruning techniques on hedges that can't be seen from the house or the main

An early morning mist transforms the dense plantings of the Norah Michener Rockery into a delicate watercolour, with its stands of asters (*Aster* 'Harrington's Pink') and two exceptional ornamental grasses, *Miscanthus sinensis* and prairie switch grass (*Panicum virgatum* 'Warrior').

The more muted tones of autumn can still be breathtaking. *Above*: A sweep of variegated phlox (*Phlox* 'Norah Leigh'), ornamental grasses (*Calamagrostis acutiflora* 'Karl Foerster'), purple coneflowers (*Echinacea purpurea*), and obedient plants (*Physostegia virginiana* 'Variegata'). The giant leaves in the background belong to the deciduous tree *Paulownia imperialis*. *Opposite*: The speckled, orchid-like bloom of the Formosan toad lily (*Tricyrtis formosana*) lives up to its common name.

gardens before they are allowed to work in the high-traffic areas. Under the skilled direction of Roeland Jansen, pruning has become an art form. The native beech hedge (*Fagus grandifolia*) along the fence of the Ambassadors' Courtyard—the courtyard on the north side of the house through which the prime minister passes whenever he pays a call on the governor general—provides but one example. When this hedge is mature, it will camouflage the fence, yet still allow visitors to see into the court. Because this species has very slow root regeneration, it takes considerable time to grow after planting. But once established, it responds remarkably well to severe pruning.

"In the autumn," says Jansen, "we cut them so they will get thicker in the centre and we always look for ways to prune so that gaps are going to be filled." The general practice these days is to prune trees with a chainsaw. In the hands of the wrong person, however, the cut is usually made too close to the trunk, removing the collar—the slight swelling at the base of the branch where it joins the trunk—and creating a large wound unlikely to heal properly. "When we use chainsaws here," Jansen adds, "we use very experienced people who are incredibly careful to avoid this problem."

When pruning, Jansen advises making a cut to the branch just above the collar, but not touching it. With the collar left in place, the tree can produce tissue to form a callus, allowing the cut to heal successfully. But he warns not to leave a stub either—it creates the perfect spot for disease to enter the system. Jansen never allows anyone on his staff to wear spikes when they are scrambling up a tree. Spikes leave holes in the trunk that become points of entry for insects and fungi.

Canadianizing the Treescape

Along with these fall rituals of any northern garden, autumn at Rideau Hall is also a time for both culling and planting trees throughout the estate, a process integral to the bedrock Canadianization policy. The number of non-native trees introduced to the property over the years has emerged as a serious problem. With no local enemies, these exotic aliens from Europe have become hugely invasive.

Above: Gardener Dagmar McCord. *Opposite*: Part of a red oak tree (*Quercus rubra*), one of hundreds of native trees planted on the Rideau Hall estate in recent years.

Jansen is directing the initiative to gradually remove a century's worth of destructive exotics, including Norway spruce (*Picea abies*), Norway maples (*Acer plantanoides*), and the common buckthorn (*Rhamnus cathartica*). We've become so used to seeing Norway maples and other foreign trees that we assume they are native. They are not.

Buckthorn is the worst offender; it will move into any niche available, elbowing aside desirable native species such as sugar maple and red oak. Because buckthorn hangs on to its leaves quite late, it is easy to identify in the autumn, but even when cut back to the ground it sends out suckers to form such dense colonies that they threaten anything growing nearby. The only solution is to remove the tree roots, while attempting not to disturb the surrounding soil and cause dormant buckthorn seeds to germinate.

On the estate as a whole, and in the sugar bush in particular, there are far too many of these unfriendly invaders for mass removal, so Jansen's strategy is to take a few down each year and heavily prune the others. Among the most successful native trees to be planted recently are hackberry (*Celtis occidentalis*) and red oak (*Quercus rubra*), both of which flourish in the loamy soil. The character of the parkland and the woodland is steadily evolving back towards earlier days.

To replace dying native trees is a particularly tricky process. Some of the maples on the grounds are well over a hundred years old and, when they die, they leave gaping holes that are particularly noticeable in the parkland areas. If a tree is visibly damaged, a new tree—usually a more shade-tolerant species such as an oak or an ironwood—is planted 9 or 10 metres away from the aging trunk. As the older tree grows more fragile, branches are removed to give the understorey tree more light and enable it to grow more quickly.

Sometimes nature itself intervenes in the culling process. The devastating ice storm that swept through eastern Ontario and Quebec in the winter of 1998-99 took with it about a third of the woodland canopy—and left some fairly big holes in the parkland. Many mature ash and elm trees collapsed, and quite a few maples were severely damaged. Only the oaks

I selected a young maple, recently planted, in a commanding position, and asked him if he would allow the tree to have the honour of being associated with his name. He descended from our motor, walked around the tree, bowed to it, and expressed himself delighted at the suggestion that the tree should be known as Prince Fushimi's tree.

LORD GREY

A view of the lower terrace in autumn shows how the ornamental grasses come into their own as the flowers fade, giving this very old garden a quite contemporary look. Massive clumps of *Miscanthus sinensis* and prairie switch grass (*Panicum virgatum* 'Warrior') hold their shape well past the first snow.

What we have attempted to create at Rideau Hall is an example of the gardening possibilities in Canada, fashioning a style that speaks of this country to gardeners all over the world.

DAGMAR MCCORD

remained relatively unscathed, including the now-massive oak planted by Charles de Gaulle in 1960, which shades the woodland garden.

Ice storm or no, the culling and replanting program continues at a steady pace. Each year, the foresters plant as many as 1,000 seedlings and ten large specimen trees, individuals that stand alone rather than being planted as part of a closer grouping. In the nursery area, usually about 100 whips (seedlings less than an inch thick) are planted for future years.

In the sugar bush, at the entrance of which is the historic skating rink area, the process of Canadianization provides perhaps the ideal metaphor for how Rideau Hall manages to honour tradition while practising contemporary gardening methods. This woodland is a vestige of what, at the time Thomas MacKay developed his country estate, was probably a mostly coniferous second-growth forest (the area around Ottawa was heavily logged in the early nineteenth century). The conifers gave way to a more deciduous mix, including sugar maples, some of which were tapped for maple syrup each spring—a practice that continues to this day. (The syrup is bottled and given away as gifts or used in the kitchen.) In the working part of the sugar bush, however, the trees are tapped only when they are mature and in top condition.

While the sugar bush is gradually being weeded of non-native species, it is also being managed as a nature sanctuary. To maintain its function as part of a flight corridor used by birds and as a habitat for animals, the foresters deliberately leave snags—partially dead trees—standing. These decaying trunks become refuges and food sources for owls, woodpeckers, and other birds, while in the long run they contribute to forest regeneration. As they decay, felled trees nurture millions of insects and become nurse logs from which new seedlings sprout. Leaving a snag or a log in place can also help prevent erosion, especially on the steep hill leading up to Rideau Hall from the sugar bush.

Among the most persistent of the invasive woodland exotics are the understorey plants that crowd out native ephemerals such as trout lilies and wild ginger. One of the most pernicious

The path through the sugar bush, which was designed for rustic nineteenth-century strolls, is still used for woodland walks. The Rideau Hall woods now provide precious habitat for many birds and mammals, acting as a nature refuge amidst the built-up area of Greater Ottawa.

of these pests is garlic mustard (*Alliaria petiolata*)—an evil little ground cover incredibly difficult to eradicate, as are Japanese knotweed (*Polygonum cuspidatum*) and wood bluegrass (*Poa nemoralis*).

Since the woodland area known collectively as the sugar bush is also a place where people stroll and which is open to the public during the annual winter party, there is an ongoing tension between what should be cleared for safety's sake and what should be left as new habitat. Slowly but surely, however, the gardeners are "getting the sugar bush back," in the words of grounds manager Mark Burleton.

Each of the gardens at Rideau Hall has its own golden moment. In spring the spotlight is on the fleeting beauty of the new woodland border. In summer the mixed perennial beds of the upper and lower terraces dazzle with their brilliant array of shimmering tones and a fascinating variety of plants. In autumn the sugar bush blazes with colour, while the staying power of the perennial garden comes to the fore: strong evergreen shapes; multicoloured bark on trees and shrubs; and great ornamental grasses whose magnificent plumes, decorated with autumn dew, gleam in the crisp fall sunlight. And when the asters, sedums, and chrysanthemums start to fade, the grasses go on shimmering well into winter.

The Rideau Hall garden is many things: a garden that fits comfortably on its site, that pays attention to local conditions, and that respects its historical roots while integrating the latest in gardening thinking. It is a garden that demonstrates the ways in which native Canadian plants can thrive in place of the tired exotics we've cultivated in the past. It is the complete twenty-first-century Canadian garden—and one that belongs to all Canadians. If a garden can be said to have a soul, this is a garden with soul to spare.

Garden Messages

We'd like to think that the gardens at Rideau Hall send a very strong message about who we are as a people at the beginning of the twenty-first century. Whether it's the thousands of trilliums that now greet visitors in early spring—emblematic Canadian flowers that have replaced the European imports—or the way the heritage of the formal garden has been uncovered and updated—the Lady Byng Rockery, for example—or in the number of northern plants we've introduced, or in the way we no longer clean up the garden in the autumn so that it's all neat and tidy and completely uninteresting. In late autumn, when the snow begins to fall on the dried grasses and late perennials and shrubs, it creates an effect of white waves, a different sort of beauty. *AC*

A perennial bed in all its autumn beauty. Below the towering monumental grass (*Miscanthus sinensis* 'Goliath') is feathery purple fountain grass (*Pennesetum setaceum* 'Rubrum'), which picks up and repeats a leitmotif that runs through the whole lower terrace. The other grasses are Japanese silver grass (*Miscanthus sinensis* 'Graziella') and *Helictotrichon*. In the foreground are yellow coneflowers (*Rudbeckia hirta*), sedums (*Sedum* 'Autumn Joy') and the wine-red blooms of *Chrysanthemum* 'Marguerite.'

SMALL SERVIETTES

PART 3

At the Nation's Table.

The chefs at Rideau Hall have attempted to create something that might be called a Canadian cuisine. When Canadians come here, you can see how proud they are that Rideau Hall is their house, showing off the country's best. What does Canada taste like? It tastes of the land. It doesn't disguise its ingredients.

by Anne L. Desjardins

CHAPTER 1

Canadian Food at Canada's House

You might say that the kitchens have become a kind of national laboratory of Canadian cooking.

Detail of an Imari plate, part of a dinner service (on loan from William and Wynn Bensen) that belonged to Sir William Van Horne, builder and first president of the Canadian Pacific Railway.

Preceding pages: Pastry chef Jérôme Dubois walks past the pots and pans in the Rideau Hall kitchen.

In the past few years something interesting has been happening in the kitchens of Rideau Hall. The food served at events, large and small, offers a vision of the country's culinary bounty.

Take, for example, the Literary Awards held in mid-November 2003 to honour the finest books in both official languages, their writing, illustration, and translation, and attended by 150 people from the world of writing, publishing, media, entertainment, and the arts in general. After the awards ceremony in the Rideau Hall Ballroom, the doors to the Reception Room were thrown open and the guests were ushered in for the first course of a spectacular dinner buffet: a magnificent selection of hors d'oeuvres set out on large mirrors, with a separate mirror for each category—vegetarian, fish and seafood, meat and poultry. The display was not only lovely to look at and delicious to taste, it constituted the first part of a pleasurable seminar on contemporary Canadian cuisine.

For the first course, the guests were offered winter black truffle and mushroom perogies; spiced capon leg stuffed with marinated root vegetables and okra; and salt-cured Arctic char rolled with lobster, Saskatchewan chanterelles, and barley and kamut (an ancient grain) salad. As the guests moved down the buffet line, they were treated to an assortment of terrines and hot and cold salads, ranging from a fall ratatouille to spicy bok choy salad to a Rideau Hall Brussels sprout salad with crisp pancetta and prairie beans.

The second course included roasted monkfish loin and stewed spicy chorizo sausage with tomato, caperberry, and onion; and a confit of Saint-Apollinaire rabbit from Quebec and Mariposa Farms duck from Ontario, with *foie gras au torchon* from Quebec. As serving staff moved among the round tables in the Tent Room, where the diners were seated, they offered a choice of a 2001 Chardonnay Reserve from Mission Hill Winery in British Columbia's Okanagan Valley and a 1998 Cabernet-Merlot from Henry of Pelham Winery in Ontario's Niagara Peninsula—fine wines from Canada's two primary wine-growing regions.

The Literary Awards dinner each year has become one of the most entertaining events at Rideau Hall. Between courses, various guests may perform impromptu readings or even sing. In November 2003 Governor General Adrienne Clarkson read a moving passage from the novel *Unless* in tribute to the memory of Carol Shields, who had recently died. Quebec poet Pierre Nepveu, the 2003 recipient for poetry, spoke about previous award winner Roland Giguère and read from his poetry. In this context, Canadian food takes on extra meaning. Before moving to dessert, the guests could taste five excellent Canadian cheeses: Capri Tomme from British Columbia, Creemore Sheep Cheese from Ontario, Ciel de Charlevoix and Petit Fleurmier from Quebec, and Le Gamin from New Brunswick.

Wild rice (*Zizania palustris*) at Sikachu Lake in northern Saskatchewan. An aquatic plant that's actually not related to the rice family, wild rice is commercially harvested from northern lakes in Ontario, Manitoba, Alberta, and especially, Saskatchewan, which alone accounts for three-quarters of Canadian production.

The desserts were all prepared with seasonal products: pumpkin-seed praline cream profiteroles; mountain cranberry Black Forest pyramid; caramel, walnut, and sun-dried apple and pear sugar torte. And these sweets were complemented by a 2001 Riesling Indian Summer Select Late Harvest from Cave Spring Winery in the Niagara Peninsula.

The guests at the Literary Awards came away impressed not only by the range and creative excellence of Canada's writers but by the artistic skills and inventiveness of Rideau Hall's kitchen brigade, not to mention the scope and variety of the foods. This evening is but one of hundreds of annual functions at Rideau Hall, ranging from small receptions for the parliamentary pages to lavish dinners for visiting heads of state, from the annual Bravery Awards to a lunch with the Multicultural Youth Council, but it demonstrates the common theme that now dominates the cuisine in our national house. At Canada's table you will be served dishes made with Canadian ingredients—foods created, raised, or picked by local, mostly small-scale producers. Here are just some of the highlights.

From the Maritimes come fiddleheads, potatoes, sea parsley, lobster and other shellfish, fine cheeses, Atlantic cod, cloudberries, and Iceberg vodka. From Quebec, Île d'Orléans capons and sturgeon caviar from Abitibi, more than three hundred specialty cheeses, wild mushrooms, foie gras, maple syrup, and crème de cassis. From Ontario, black walnuts, hazelnuts, almonds, apples, peaches, plums, and even figs, organic greens, goat cheese, aged cheddar, and wild ginger. From the three Prairie provinces, grains, Saskatoon berries, lamb, beef and bison, wild garlic and wild rice, organic colza oil, birch syrup, cattail hearts, marinated daisy capers, Parmesan-style cheese, and some exceptional goat cheese. From British Columbia, wild Pacific salmon, Haida Gwaii shrimp, red snapper, line-caught tuna, northern black cod, wild mushrooms (including the rare pine mushrooms of Bella Coola), tiny oolichans, goat and sheep cheese from Saltspring Island, sumac and salal berries, cherries, apricots, and pistachios. Finally, from the Far North, caribou, muskox, Arctic char, and teas made from northern plants and berries. Accompanying every course, from appetizers to desserts, are wines from the Okanagan and Niagara.

Some of the best food and the best wine from Canada's regions make their way to Rideau Hall, but that is only the beginning. You might say that the kitchens have become a kind of national laboratory of Canadian cooking. Here, executive chef Oliver Bartsch and executive sous-chef Louis Charest, along with their talented team, create unique dishes that mirror the diverse flavours of the country. They see it as a calling to prepare fine food that reflects their country.

And it already seems completely natural to showcase Canadian food and Canadian wine at Canada's House. You might say it is a form of nationalism—gastronomic nationalism—which sends out a very positive message.

Sending a Message

In a sense, everything we do at Rideau Hall is about sending a message—and one of the strongest messages we send is with the food we serve. First of all, the food is superb, thanks to Oliver and Louis and their team. But their skill would be wasted if they were trying to imitate food from somewhere else. Instead, they seek out the best and the freshest products from both the Ottawa area and across the country. And they invent new dishes all the time to show off all these ingredients. Then we tell our guests what they're eating, where it's from, who made it, and so on.

When Canadians come here, it changes their view of Canada. You can see how proud they are that Rideau Hall is their house, showing off the country's best stuff. Serving Canadian wine and Canadian food prepared by Canadian chefs is a powerful statement of self-confidence. It's a way of reminding ourselves that Canadians are achieving levels of excellence that are equal to anything, anywhere.

You can't measure the impact, but you can begin to imagine how this works when you have people from farther away over for dinner—ambassadors and presidents and prime ministers. It opens their eyes to Canada in the twenty-first century. *AC*

Portraits of Canadian bounty (*left to right*): Cows grazing near Plessisville, Quebec, in the Bois-Francs region of the St. Lawrence Lowland, an area renowned for its dairy products, including a number of fine cheeses, and its maple syrup; landscape near Arctic Bay, Nunavut, where the Inuit, by being careful not to overfish, operate a sustainable commercial fishery; a field of Manitoba flax, one of nature's richest sources of antioxidants and essential fatty acids.

The Ball-Room ; Government House.
arranged for a Parliamentary Dinner of 100 Guests.

Above: Menu cover from the farewell dinner held in honour of Lord Aberdeen, governor general from 1893 to 1898. *Opposite*: The Ballroom set for a parliamentary dinner in the 1880s (during a subsequent expansion of the house the large windows were closed in and replaced with mirrors). The table in the shape of an elongated horseshoe was typical for state dinners until fairly recently. Now smaller round tables allow guests to have conversations with those seated across from them as well as with their immediate neighbours.

A Brief History

It may seem natural that Canadian food would be showcased at Government House, the residence of Canada's head of state and the meeting place for people from across Canada as well as dignitaries from around the world. Until relatively recently, however, this was not the case.

The early governors general were British aristocrats accustomed to elaborate, multi-course meals in the European mode. The British Empire was at its peak, and the proconsuls of the empire wanted only the "best" of foods on their table. For them, that meant French food and French wine. Whether the chefs they brought with them were French or not, French culinary traditions dominated. A glance at the menus for meals served at Rideau Hall from the 1890s until late in the twentieth century reveals that classic French cuisine and French wine were served almost exclusively, a custom that didn't change even after Vincent Massey, the first Canadian-born governor general, took office in 1952.

But outside the gates of Rideau Hall, Canada was evolving. Its population was becoming more diverse and its chefs more self-confident and original. By the late 1980s a new generation of young Canadian cooks trained in the classical French manner were exploring their own country's roots. At the same time, almost unnoticed except by a few enthusiasts, Canadian wine was developing a level of excellence.

Carte Blanche

Adrienne Clarkson arrived as governor general, along with her husband, John Ralston Saul, at an opportune moment, one when our native cuisine was coming into its own. They gave the chefs at Rideau Hall carte blanche to use products from every part of the country. According to executive chef Oliver Bartsch, who brought the fresh thinking with him when he joined the Rideau Hall kitchen as executive sous-chef during the previous mandate, they instantly communicated their passion for advocating Canadian food, "which was a source of inspiration. They encouraged us to explore every aspect of Canada's gastronomic identity."

By 1999 Canadian chefs could choose from an impressive range of home-grown fruits, grains, vegetables, meats, and poultry, more than 400 specialty artisan cheeses, and wines from some 120 vintners producing quality-controlled wines. And this extraordinary richness did not just suddenly appear. Until recently, Canada was not noted for its food, though we have long been known as the breadbasket of the world and for our superb western beef. Of course, there were certain regional specialties—Nova Scotia fish chowder, Quebec tourtière, breaded Georgian Bay whitefish, pan-fried Lake Winnipeg goldeye, saskatoon berry jams, fresh Dungeness crab from British Columbia—but nothing resembling a true regional cuisine. This local richness is something that developed, little by little, as professional Canadian cooks began to demand more of themselves and of local producers.

In the late 1980s many of our more adventurous chefs came under the influence of the Slow Food Movement, which chose its name in opposition to fast food and all it stands for. The movement began in Italy, where a handful of culinary activists decided to counter the widespread obsession with instant gratification as well as the excesses of fusion cuisine, whose extreme proponents scoured the hemispheres for rare or exotic ingredients, heedless of the environmental costs. The Slow Food Movement promotes smaller-scale, sustainable agriculture with roots in local communities. It strives to respect the rhythms of the seasons and to recover traditional foods and methods that are in danger of being lost in the rush

Home Cooking

Every country has an approach to eating and drinking that goes to the heart of the place—its geography, its climate, its history, the kind of society it is. In Italy, for instance, an old civilization where the regionalism is strong, the way of cooking is all about seasons and natural products and letting the flavours of the individual ingredients come through. When you take into account our aboriginal peoples, the roots of Canadian cooking go back at least as far as the Italian.

Canada occupies the second-largest land mass of any country in the world and boasts an incredible range of climate zones, soils, and habitats. It's also now home to people who've come from every part of the globe and adapted their cooking to the place they live in. (Think of the wonderful aged Gouda from Alberta—originally a Dutch cheese.) The cuisine that's emerging here is about regions, good ingredients, strong flavours—and very definite seasons!

Partly because of immigration patterns, but above all because of the size of the country, each region has its own food traditions and traditional dishes. Every cook, no matter from where in the country, has these wonderful sources to work with, and more and more people are demanding local, seasonal products. *JRS*

Oliver Bartsch (*right*) and Louis Charest prepare a spiced apple–rosemary meringue dessert for a culinary event to be held in Stratford, Ontario. Under the leadership of Bartsch and Charest, the kitchens at Rideau Hall have been transformed into a laboratory of fine Canadian cooking.

Louis Charest
Sous-Chef
Rideau Hall

towards homogenization and globalization. It celebrates local produce and espouses a return to culinary simplicity, insisting on cooking that demands the highest quality of individual ingredients while allowing their fresh flavours to shine through. It recognizes the importance of terroir.

The term terroir is well known to people who work with wine. It refers to the soils and the microclimate of a specific vineyard that give unique characteristics to a particular wine. More and more, however, the term is also being used to describe the unique qualities of food from a specific region. Lamb from the Charlevoix region of Quebec tastes different from lamb from Saltspring Island in British Columbia because each reflects its own distinct terroir.

In the 1980s a growing number of Canadian chefs embraced the philosophy of supporting and working with local producers while asking more and more of them. As a result of this process, we are beginning to see a repopulation and rejuvenation of many dying agricultural communities. Each time a renowned chef agreed to buy a small producer's organic vegetables or goat cheese or free-range chicken, that farmer's chance of staying in business increased. When the same chef told other chefs and patrons about these local products, their producers found new customers. But there's another significant result of this symbiosis between individual chef and local producer: better and more varied produce. The chef may do some research, then pass it along to the producer. Or the producer may introduce a new variety, perhaps an heirloom tomato, that will find a sure buyer in the local chef. The chef may ask for something that can't yet be found in the region, and the small producer will attempt to fill the gap.

Thanks to this partnership, many heirloom vegetables have been reintroduced to our tables, and a large number of artisan cheeses are being produced in almost every province. Superb organically raised meats and poultry are proving that natural—without pesticides, additives, growth hormones, and chemical fertilizers—is healthier, better tasting, more nutritious, and more environmentally friendly. Today the exponents of this "common-sense culinary revolution" are active right across

Mushroom medley (*clockwise from top left*): a fairy ring mushroom, black trumpets, yellow foot chanterelles, cinnamon caps, and chanterelles. All but the cinnamon caps (greenhouse-grown in Quebec) are wild mushrooms from British Columbia, but they can also be found in many other parts of Canada.

the country. Many of them have taken on the role of educators, explaining to anyone who will listen the importance of fresh ingredients, grown or raised without damaging the environment. They insist on the importance of producing quality foods at a fair price, and on the role such foods play in improving our diet and our health.

These daring and creative chefs may be separated by thousands of kilometres, but they belong to a passionate fraternity that shares a simple philosophy: to highlight the best that their country offers by creating a cuisine that is seasonal and local. They include the likes of Sinclair Philip (Sooke Harbour House, Vancouver Island), David Hawksworth (West, Vancouver), Michael Stadtländer (Eigensinn Farm, Ontario), Mark McEwan (North 44, Toronto), Jamie Kennedy (Jamie Kennedy Wine Bar, Toronto), Susur Lee (Susur, Toronto), Normand Laprise (Toqué! Montreal), Anne Desjardins, no relation to me (L'eau à la Bouche, in the Laurentians), Dennis Johnson (Fid, Halifax), and Michael Smith (Prince Edward Island). And among their number are now the executive chef and the executive sous-chef at Rideau Hall: Oliver Bartsch and Louis Charest.

When the Whole Country Is Your Terroir

Supporting local businesses right across the country was as critical to the new Governor General and her husband as was their belief in Rideau Hall's role as a showcase for Canadian food, Canadian wine, and Canadian cooking. And they challenged the chefs at Rideau Hall to reflect the whole country in their cooking, without simply paying lip service to its different parts. They wanted them to encompass in their kitchens a land covering nearly 10 million square kilometres, the margins of three oceans, and countless freshwater lakes and rivers—including many different regions, to say nothing of one of the world's most diverse populations.

Naturally and logically, the chefs at Canada's House began working with their own region, the Ottawa Valley—starting with their organic garden, where fresh herbs and vegetables are harvested from early spring to late fall. They joined their

Wild ingredients are often used in Rideau Hall dishes (*clockwise from top left*): cloudberries, or bakeapple; sea chickweed; black locust flower syrup (in top of split bowl); wild rose petals (in bottom); salmonberries (in the spoon); red huckleberries; ox-eye daisy capers; cattail hearts (in the square dish). Because our seasons are so extreme and the divisions between them so sharp, our home-grown foods are very different from season to season.

fellow Ottawa-Gatineau area chefs in encouraging a diversified network of local producers. At Boucanerie Chelsea, just north of Ottawa, for instance, they can stock up on locally caught smoked fish. They have established a solid partnership with a network of local organic growers, including Bryson Farms of Shawville, Ontario, producers of organic microgreens, and Fines herbes par Daniel from Val-des-Monts in the Outaouais just outside of Gatineau, growers of edible flowers and greens.

The Rideau Hall terroir includes small producers of exclusively grain-fed beef as well as farms that raise Muscovy duck, quail, pheasant, organic grain-fed chicken, and fresh lamb. They have also established a partnership with the millers from Mountain Path, 50 kilometres south of Ottawa, producers and distributors of a large variety of organic grains, flours, and legumes. Outside their immediate region, they can order a vast selection of rare vegetables from Cookstown Greens, David Cohlmeyer's 20-hectare farm near Toronto. The produce includes mini beets, salsify (a small root vegetable), fingerling potatoes, parsley root, purple carrots, and mesclun—a mix of salad greens.

Up to this point, the chefs at Rideau Hall are working in the same way as many of the country's other top chefs: creating a truly regional cuisine. By definition, Canadian regional cuisine has its basis in specific microclimates and the food products unique to that region. David Hawksworth from Vancouver, for instance, may feature wild Pacific salmon,

How Does Canada Taste?

Whether we're talking about a banquet at Rideau Hall or a meal you might serve your family or your guests at home, you have a choice. You can explore and take pleasure in food from someplace else or you can celebrate the place you're from with all its individual flavours. By choosing to seek out food and drink that comes from your place, you say something very positive.

All food comes from somewhere. And if you knowingly choose your own country's products when you create a meal, the meal becomes an expression of the place you are from. Serving Canadian food cooked in a Canadian way by Canadian cooks is actually an old-fashioned kind of belonging. It says that we come from somewhere, we understand what that place is, and we're proud to be from there.

What it all comes down to is respect for ingredients. What is emerging is a Canadian palate and a Canadian cuisine obsessed with product. You can see that when you go around the country and taste what the good young chefs are cooking. Respect for ingredients means knowing where something comes from, who grew or raised it, and preparing it so that its natural flavours come through.

What does the country taste like? It tastes of the land. It doesn't disguise its ingredients or where they come from. Its flavours are incredibly varied, and they taste strong and true. *AC*

Organic vegetables harvested from the Rideau Hall vegetable garden (*clockwise from top left*): candy cane beet, lemon grass, bull's blood beet (the dark beet in the middle), fingerling potatoes, white turnip, mini green courgettes (zucchini), purple carrot, sunburst yellow squash, Chiogga beet, red carrots, and yellow carrot.

The food I ate as a kid growing up in Ottawa was both Canadian and Chinese. We always had a Canadian breakfast and a Canadian lunch. But for dinner, I would say five times out of seven, we had a Cantonese home-cooked meal.

ADRIENNE CLARKSON

Princess Royal Island lingcod, raspberries and blackberries from the Fraser Valley, cheese or lamb from Saltspring Island, and peaches and wines from the Okanagan Valley. Almost 5,000 kilometres to the east, colleague Normand Laprise of Montreal might base his menu on Boileau venison, quails or pheasant from Cap-Saint-Ignace, organic vegetables grown by Pierre-André Daignault in the Laurentians, or goat cheese from La Chèvrerie Tournevent in the Bois-Francs region.

For the chefs at Rideau Hall, however, the whole country is their terroir. Their mandate is to celebrate the best that this national terroir can provide. They supplement the harvest of their local region in ever-widening circles that will eventually encompass all of Canada—and that means getting to know the country's edible resources. It has led them to begin to define the characteristics of Canadian food.

Canada is a northern country with a northern climate that dictates what we can grow. Here, the notion of seasons is primordial. During the harvest season we still stock up on preserves, jams, and jellies in preparation for the long winter to come. Then there is the country's sheer size and the spaces it provides for free-ranging game, including bison, deer, and caribou. Along with size and space comes an abundance of edible wild fruits and other wild plants we have learned to harvest, a precious heritage from our First Nations. There is the wealth of our waters, both salt and fresh. And, finally, there is Canada's cultural diversity, which provides a host of culinary traditions on which to draw. Based on these broad principles, Rideau Hall has attempted to create something that might be called a Canadian cuisine.

The fixings of a Rideau Hall salad (*clockwise from top left*): chervil, arugula, China rose radish seedlings, micro Swiss chard seedlings, frisée (endive), dill, white dandelion, lollarossa, and red cabbage sprouts. The chefs either harvest these from their vegetable garden or buy them locally, but all are available right across the country.

Amuse-Bouche of Vodka-Cured Salmon with Tomato and Scallion Salad and Pea Purée

This dish is similar to gravlax, with its traditional salt-and-sugar curing, but when prepared at Rideau Hall, it is cured with East Coast (Iceberg) vodka, then garnished with wild pickled ginger salad.

At Rideau Hall the chefs use only wild salmon. Unlike farmed salmon, wild salmon is more muscular and less fatty. Before preparing this recipe, allow 48 hours to cure the salmon, making sure to turn the fillets every 12 hours, if possible.

Suggested wine: Sumac Ridge Stellers Jay Brut

Serves 4

for salmon

1 lb (450 g) whole boneless salmon fillet, with skin
1/4 cup (62 mL) granulated sugar
2 tbsp (30 mL) coarse sea salt
2 shallots, finely chopped
4 sprigs rosemary, finely chopped
2 tsp (10 mL) honey
1/4 cup (62 mL) vodka
1 tsp (5 mL) crushed black peppercorns

for salad

1 wild scallion or 2 regular scallions
1 roma or vine-ripened tomato
1 tbsp (15 mL) white balsamic vinegar
2 tbsp (30 mL) vodka
2 tbsp (30 mL) extra-virgin olive oil
1 tbsp (15 mL) packed brown sugar

for pea purée

1 cup (250 mL) fresh green peas
1 tbsp (15 mL) heavy cream
1 tsp (5 mL) crème fraîche or sour cream (optional)
pinch granulated sugar
salt and white pepper

for salmon

Using a sharp knife, slice the salmon fillet into 2 pieces lengthwise and place on a small baking tray or container, flesh-side up.

In a small bowl, stir the sugar and salt together; set aside. In another bowl, mix together the shallots, rosemary, honey, and pepper, then set aside.

Sprinkle the vodka over the salmon fillets, then sprinkle the salt-and-sugar mixture and finally the shallot-and-honey mixture, ensuring that both fillets are evenly coated.

Presentation

Spoon some purée onto each plate, place a portion of salad next to the purée, and artfully arrange a few slices of the cured salmon around the plate.

Place one fillet flesh-side down over the other. Wrap the salmon tightly in plastic wrap and place on a platter or cutting board. Place a flat, heavy weight (such as a chopping board or small cast-iron frying pan) on top of the wrapped fish and refrigerate for 2 days. Every 12 hours or so, turn the wrapped fillets over and reapply the weight.

When the salmon is cured, remove the wrap and, using your fingers, brush off the curing mixture so that no salt and sugar remain. Slice thinly and set aside.

for salad

Slice the scallions into fine strips or quarters, no more than 1 1⁄2 inch long. Place in a medium bowl and set aside.

Meanwhile, cut the tomato in half. Dry the halves in the oven for 1 1⁄2 to 2 hours for a normal oven at 300°F (150°C) or 45 minutes to 1 hour at 300°F (150°C) for a convection oven. Remove the tomato from the oven and slice into thin strips. Add the strips to the scallion.

In a separate bowl, mix together the vinegar, vodka, olive oil, and brown sugar to make a dressing. Pour the dressing over the scallion-and-tomato mixture and marinate for 1 hour.

for pea purée

In a pot of boiling salted water, blanch the peas for 2 minutes. Remove from the heat and drain. Purée the peas in a food processor until they are smooth. Place the puréed peas in a medium bowl. Add the cream, salt, white pepper, and sugar. Mix well. Cover the mixture and refrigerate for 1 hour. If you are using the crème fraîche or sour cream, fold it in just before serving and adjust the seasoning to taste.

Boletus Mushroom, Scallion, and Potato Salad in a Warm Thyme Crème de Cassis Vinaigrette

The boletus is a wild mushroom that the chefs of Rideau Hall picked while on a visit to La Malbaie, in the Charlevoix region of Quebec. Another wild mushroom favoured by the chefs is the lobster mushroom, so called because of its red skin. It has a meaty texture and holds its shape well when it's steamed or blanched. If neither one is available, substitute shiitake mushrooms. Any cassis syrup or product could be substituted for the crème de cassis.

The two major suppliers of wild mushrooms are Quebec and British Columbia, though an abundance of fresh mushrooms grown by small producers from across the country is available in markets and some specialty stores.

Suggested wine: Quail's Gate Pinot Noir Family Reserve

Serves 4

for vinaigrette

1⁄4 cup (62 mL) extra-virgin olive oil
3 tbsp (45 mL) crème de cassis
1 tbsp (15 mL) red wine vinegar
1 tbsp (15 mL) peeled and finely chopped shallots
1 tbsp (15 mL) chopped fresh thyme
salt and cracked black peppercorns

for salad

2 cups (500 mL) sliced boletus or shiitake mushrooms
1⁄4 cup (62 mL) chopped scallions
2 cups (500 mL) quartered Viking red potatoes or other small red-skinned potatoes
1 tbsp (15 mL) chopped fresh thyme
1 tbsp (15 mL) cracked black peppercorns
salt

In a medium bowl, add the oil, crème de cassis, wine vinegar, shallots, and thyme; whisk them together until the dressing begins to emulsify. Season with salt and pepper and set aside.

Bring a large pot of salted water to a boil and either blanch the mushrooms for 2 minutes or steam them for 1 minute. If blanching, remove the mushrooms from the water and cool them in an ice bath; if steaming, remove the mushrooms from the heat and set aside.

Meanwhile, in the same pot, bring the water back to a boil and add the potatoes. Boil them for approximately 10 to 15 minutes or until tender. Drain the potatoes and sprinkle them with vinaigrette, thyme, salt, and pepper.

In a bowl, mix together the potatoes, mushrooms, scallions, thyme, and vinaigrette. Adjust the seasoning to taste, garnish with thyme seedlings, and serve.

Prosciutto-Wrapped Pickerel and Warm Sweet Potato–Bean Salad

Wild pickerel is used in this recipe, but any white fish will do. Here the mixture of the subtle-flavoured pickerel and the pungent, salty prosciutto makes for an interesting contrast in texture, flavour, and colour. The bell peppers in the Spanish-inspired romesco sauce give the dish a Mediterranean feel and a multicultural delight.

Suggested wine: Jackson-Triggs Chardonnay Delaine Vineyards

Serves 4

for pickerel

1 1/2 lb (675 g) fresh pickerel fillet, skinned and boned
6 ounces (170 g) prosciutto, thinly sliced
2 shallots, finely chopped
juice of one lemon
1 tbsp (15 mL) chopped flat-leaf parsley
salt and pepper
1 tbsp (15 mL) olive oil

for salad

4 pearl onions, peeled and halved
2 shallots, finely chopped
4 cloves garlic, chopped
1/8 cup (31 mL) cooked or canned soybeans
1/4 cup (62 mL) cooked or canned fava beans
1/4 cup (62 mL) cooked or canned white beans
1/4 cup (62 mL) cooked or canned lima beans
1/4 cup (62 mL) cooked or canned pinto beans
1/2 cup (125 mL) diced sweet potato, cooked until almost tender
zest of 1/2 lemon
juice of 1/2 lemon
1/4 cup (62 mL) white balsamic vinegar or rice wine vinegar
1/2 cup (125 mL) canola oil
2 tbsp (30 mL) chopped fresh chives
2 sprigs fresh tarragon

for romesco sauce

1/2 cup (125 mL) roasted pine nuts or almonds (see sidebar)
1/4 tsp (1 mL) chili flakes or smoked paprika
6 roasted garlic cloves (see sidebar)
1 sweet red pepper, roasted and skinned
2 roma tomatoes, oven baked (see sidebar)
pinch salt
3 to 4 tbsp (45 to 60 mL) red wine vinegar
1 cup (250 mL) extra-virgin olive oil

To roast pine nuts: place the nuts on a baking sheet and bake at 350°F (175°C) for approximately 10 minutes or until they are toasted golden brown.

To roast garlic: place a whole garlic bulb, with its skin, on a sheet of foil. Add a bit of olive oil and kosher salt, rub them over the garlic bulb, and wrap. Place the package in a 375°F (190°C) oven and leave for 45 minutes or until the garlic can be easily squeezed out of its skin. The garlic should be soft, slightly browned or caramelized, and sweet in flavour.

To oven-bake tomatoes: slice the tomatoes in half. Place the halves on a baking sheet, brush with olive oil, and sprinkle with kosher salt. Bake in a 375°F (190°C) oven for approximately 35 minutes or until the halves are slightly caramelized yet still moist.

Presentation

When serving, spoon the warm bean salad onto the plates. Place the fish over the salad and drizzle it with the pan juices. Spoon romesco sauce around each salad and serve. A nice finishing touch would be some seasoned microgreens, which add a lovely texture to this dish.

for pickerel

Trim the fillets into 8 equal portions. Lay them on a tray, fleshy side up. Season with the shallots, lemon juice, parsley, salt, and pepper. To make 4 portions, place one pickerel fillet over another so that the seasoned sides meet. Wrap each portion with a thin slice of prosciutto: be sure that the prosciutto ends overlap, to maintain a seal when cooking.

When ready to serve, add oil to a frying pan and heat on medium-high. Pan-sear each portion 2 minutes for each side. (Sear the seam side first to ensure a proper seal.) Season with salt and pepper and set aside.

for salad

Preheat the oven to 400°F (205°C). In an oven-proof frying pan, sear the onion halves in canola oil for 3 minutes or until they appear to be slightly caramelized. Remove the frying pan from the stovetop and place it in the oven for 10 minutes or until the onion is soft.

In a large saucepan, heat the oil on medium-high. Add the shallots and garlic and sauté for 3 minutes or until translucent. Add the beans, onion halves, sweet potato, zest, lemon juice, vinegar, and canola oil. Bring to a simmer, then cook for 2 minutes more to allow the flavours to infuse the liquid. Season with chives and tarragon and set aside.

Just before serving, return the pot to the stove and reheat for 2 minutes or until it is warmed.

for sauce

In a mortar and pestle, or using a food processor, grind together the roasted pine nuts, chilies, garlic, and salt. Add the roasted pepper and oven-baked tomatoes and grind to a smooth paste. Add the vinegar. Slowly incorporate the olive oil, adding a drop of water halfway through as the sauce emulsifies. Adjust the seasoning to taste.

Ontario Woodlands Wild Ginger and Roasted Niagara Plum Crème Brûlée

Our eastern woodlands are full of wild ginger, a wonderful root vegetable. The wild ginger harvest begins even before the snow has melted because it comes up underneath the snow—early proof that spring is coming. You can easily grow it in your backyard, and it's now one of the underplantings in Rideau Hall's woodland garden. The chefs use it in a variety of desserts, including a wild-ginger chocolate recipe, this crème brûlée, and too many savoury dishes to name. Whenever someone dining at Rideau Hall remarks on any one of these delicious desserts or dishes, the chefs will always credit the Canadian ginger.

Suggested wine: Inniskillin Riesling Icewine

Serves 4

- 2 cups (500 mL) heavy cream
- 1 cup (250 mL) finely chopped wild ginger
- 5 egg yolks
- 2⁄3 cup (165 mL) granulated sugar
- 4 plums, diced
- 1 tbsp (15 mL) melted unsalted butter

In a heavy-bottomed saucepot on medium-high heat, add the cream and slowly bring to a boil. Add the wild ginger and cover. Remove the pot from the heat and set it aside for at least 1 hour to infuse the cream. Once the cream is infused, strain it through a fine sieve and set aside.

In a large mixing bowl, lightly beat the yolks and all but 2 tbsp (30 mL) of the sugar until creamy. With a wooden spoon or spatula, slowly incorporate the infused cream. Meanwhile, in a medium sauté pan, sear the plums for 2 minutes with the butter and the sugar. Remove the plums from the heat and divide them into four 5-ounce (150 mL) ramekins.

Preheat the oven to 300°F (150°C). Pour the cream mixture into the ramekins. Place the ramekins in a bain-marie (a 2-inch-high baking pan containing 1 inch of water), put it in the oven, and bake for about 1 hour or until a skin has formed on the surface. Remove the ramekins from the bain-marie and allow them to cool. Once cooled, place them in the refrigerator for at least 4 to 6 hours or until they are set.

When ready to serve, remove the ramekins from the refrigerator and sprinkle the remaining 2 tbsp (30 mL) of sugar on the surface to form a thin layer. Heat with a torch or under the broiler until the sugar melts and caramelizes. Serve immediately.

CHAPTER 2

Cooking with Canada's Culinary Heritage From these diverse sources, the chefs at Rideau Hall create contemporary dishes and whole menus that reflect and celebrate our pluralistic society.

Detail of a fragment of a Haida totem pole from Skidegate, BC, on loan from the Canadian Museum of Civilization. It shows part of a high-relief carving of a grizzly bear with raised paws, protruding tongue, and curled nose.

Learning from Our First Cooks

Schoolchildren learn the story of how Jacques Cartier and his crew were saved from scurvy by members of the Iroquois Nation who showed them how to prepare a tea made from white cedar, which turns out to be rich in vitamin C. Yet few Canadians are aware of the rich culinary legacy we have inherited from the original inhabitants of Canada. The native peoples taught the European settlers how to adapt to the rigours of a harsh climate and the sharp transitions between seasons, and how to make the best use of the brief growing season in most parts of the country. They showed them how to grow corn, squash, and beans (the "three sisters"), where to harvest cranberries and other wild fruits, and the way to make a delicious syrup by boiling down the sap of the sugar maple in spring. They showed them how to harvest the wild rice that grows in northern lakes by carefully beating the stalks into a container in a canoe, while leaving the plant intact for the next season, and how to cure this grain by drying it slowly in the open air and the sun—a method still used today. They taught them that some wild berries, such as pembina, or high-bush cranberries, were not only edible but medicinally beneficial (they too are rich in vitamin C). And they knew that pembina fruit, while very sour, sweetens after the first frost.

Until a short time ago, however, much of this traditional knowledge was neglected, and some of it has been lost. In recent years First Nations chefs such as David Wolfman of the Xaxli'p Nation in British Columbia and Arnold Olson of the Cree Nation in northern Saskatchewan have helped us to rediscover an impressive culinary heritage. Olson focuses on reviving traditional native cuisine and has created dishes such as Three Sisters Soup, a delicious combination of corn, beans, and squash. These vegetables were typically grown together in a sustainable way: the beans climbed on the corn stalks and returned nitrogen to the soil, while the low-growing squash vines shaded all the roots and kept weeds from sprouting. Wolfman, in contrast, concentrates on creating aboriginal

Nature's harvest (*left to right*): harvesting seaweed at Dark Harbour on Grand Manaan Island in the Bay of Fundy; freshly picked wild blueberries, one of only four fruits native to North America; chicken-of-the-woods mushroom. The seaweed being harvested here is nori, which tastes a bit like bubblegum before it is dried (this type of seaweed is used for sushi and to wrap fresh fruits and vegetables). One-quarter of the North American production of blueberries (including both wild and cultivated kinds) comes from eastern Canada: PEI, Newfoundland, New Brunswick, and Quebec. When cooked, the chicken-of-the-woods mushroom actually tastes something like lemony chicken. It is particularly good in a vegetarian risotto.

recipes with a modern twist. He might, for example, prepare a stew of curried caribou or make moose-meat cabbage rolls.

Oliver Bartsch and Louis Charest believe our First Nations culinary legacy is one of the most important facets of a truly Canadian cuisine. And, thanks to a number of native-run businesses, many traditional ingredients have become available in recent years. For example, shrimp, turbot, and Arctic char come from Pangnirtung Fisheries in Nunavut; muskox, a relatively unknown meat that is leaner and more tender than beef, is provided by the hunters of Kitkmeot, also in Nunavut; caribou comes from Kivalliq Arctic Foods in Rankin Inlet, Nunavut; and Inuit teas and Nordic shrimp are shipped south from the Makivik Co-operative of Nunavik.

Moose Five Ways

It used to be that whenever the governor general came to town, people figured, "Well, we're entertaining a bigshot from the big city, so we'd better put on a fancy meal like he or she would eat at home." And they ended up serving meals that had nothing to do with their place, their town, or their region. Now when you go to St. John's or Iqaluit or Red Deer or Prince George, you get local food—and it's incredibly good!

One of the most memorable meals I've eaten was in the Yukon. It consisted almost entirely of moose: boiled moose, roasted moose, moose stew, moose loaf, and, the last part, moose fried rice. It was superb, because moose was the only meat. A Canadian chef in the south would probably have called it "Moose Five Ways."

I don't generally eat much meat, but there is nothing like wild game. At a wonderful outdoor feast given by the Dene people in Fort Simpson in the Northwest Territories, they served caribou spareribs, barbecued and crispy, as well as moose stew and lake trout and whitefish and bannock. When our native people give a feast, it really is a feast. If you ate the way they did traditionally, I think you'd be very healthy. *AC*

These days, almost every Rideau Hall menu includes an element of First Nations food used in original ways or in unexpected combinations. The slow-roasted Manitoba bison tenderloin served at an Order of Canada dinner in 2003 was accompanied by a wild rice risotto—an indigenous New World ingredient prepared in an Old World way. Sometimes the chefs create more complex dishes that combine a number of First Nations elements—for example, a caribou and muskox potée, or ragout, in a broth infused with Inuit herbal tea. More often they create dishes incorporating a number of native and non-native ingredients. At a 2003 dinner for the ambassadors from circumpolar countries (Norway, Sweden, Finland, Denmark, Iceland, Russia), the main dish was a pan-seared Canadian turbot fillet flavoured with sumac, a bitter spice made from the sumac bush. The fish was served on a plate with buttered Swiss chard (which flourishes in our climate) and a stir-fry of salmonberry, fiddleheads, and morel mushrooms.

The Rideau Hall chefs seldom get the chance to visit native communities, but the governor general does—it goes with the job. Adrienne Clarkson and John Ralston Saul have visited every region of the country during their mandate, and paid special attention to First Nations communities. Bartsch and Charest recall with amusement how the Governor General and her husband often returned from a trip with some culinary discovery. After a visit to Haida Gwaii (the Queen Charlotte Islands), they brought back some oolichans, oily fish resembling sardines that the coastal First Nations have traditionally eaten as a kind of high-protein canapé. (They first ate oolichans while staying at David Phillips's bed and breakfast on Haida Gwaii.) On a visit to Manitoba a Cree woman named Mary Richard gave them her recipe for pemmican, the traditional long-lasting staple of the itinerant Plains

Freshly caught Arctic char drying on the shore of Rankin Inlet, Nunavut. Char, a member of the salmon family, is by far the most important fish resource for people from Nunavut and is still part of the traditional way of life. It is also important to the local economy as a game fish that draws anglers from around the world because of its combativeness.

Indians, made of a mixture of dehydrated bison meat and dried fruit.

The kitchen team welcomed these unfamiliar ingredients and new ideas with relish. Before long, they began showing up on the menu.

Tasting Canada's Cultural Diversity

Canada today is much more than the sum of its three founding peoples—the First Nations, the French, and the British—but these three traditions are threads that continue to run through Canadian cooking. Most noticeable, in addition to the native influence, is the legacy of New France, a legacy especially obvious in the intensive use of culinary techniques such as slow roasting and braising meats by young Quebec and Acadian chefs, in the abundant use of root vegetables during the cold season, and in the rediscovery of old grains and flours such as sarrazin and rye. This French-Canadian heritage also manifests itself in the use of a number of wild foods—cattail hearts, daisy capers, and berries—which the early settlers learned about from the native peoples.

Canada in the twenty-first century has become a multicultural country, a nation of different people from many different places. From these diverse sources, the chefs at Rideau Hall create contemporary dishes and whole menus that reflect and celebrate our pluralistic society. When Oliver Bartsch and his team cook for the thousands of guests who come to Rideau Hall each year, they constantly borrow from a variety of

Oolichans

At almost every event in Haida Gwaii, there'll be a bowl of smoked oolichans. An oolichan (also spelled "eulachon" and quite a few other ways) is a fish about 20 centimetres long that's a very oily type of smelt—a distant relative of the Pacific salmon—that has for thousands of years been an important part of the highly developed culture of the First Nations people of British Columbia. Think of it as solidified fish oil. It's also known as the candlefish or lampfish because it retains so much oil it could be used for lamps. They are eaten in many ways, but I find them delicious when they're smoked. One of the best ways to eat them is at room temperature. You just pick up the head between your thumb and forefinger and start eating from the tail until you've eaten the whole thing.

The interesting point is that when you eat an oolichan you're not just eating something delicious and local that's been smoked and consumed for hundreds of years, you're eating a piece of Canadian history. Because the oolichan was the densest in oil of all the Northwest Coast fish species, it was the most valuable—so valuable that it became a form of currency. Oolichans were a major source of winter vitamins and the oil could be used for cooking fuel as well as for lamps. If the first Europeans had tried eating a few oolichans instead of boiling their meat out of existence, a lot fewer of them would have died of scurvy.

When we serve smoked oolichans and scrambled eggs to guests at Rideau Hall, we tell them they're eating something that represents west-coast Canadian history. That's often the beginning of a conversation about the complex relationships among the First Nations in the Pacific Northwest, and the complex mythology that lay beneath the simple imperatives of survival. *JRS*

Smoked oolichans on Tsimshian drying racks in the 1920s. This oil-dense fish is still a delicacy among Northwest Coast First Nations. It is also healthy: the oil is rich in iodine and many essential vitamins and minerals. As well as being used for fuel, the oil was used to preserve fruit and eaten with fresh fruit as a dessert.

traditions. They may take an ethnic dish like an East European perogy but fill it with smoked sturgeon from the Outaouais and caviar from Abitibi instead of the traditional potatoes or cheese. And the classic Russian beef stroganoff becomes a bison stroganoff, with wild Canadian mushrooms.

At the Governor General's Youth Forum held in February 2002, for example, the chefs created an eclectic series of dishes to impress the young participants with the richness of our many cultures: Latin American quesadillas made with Manitoba bison and Balderson cheddar cheese; grilled grain-fed chicken from the Prairies; and grilled Haida Gwaii shrimp served with a spicy ginger hoisin barbeque sauce rooted in classic Chinese cuisine. These dishes are not relics of our colonial past, but reflect Canada today.

When the King and Queen of Norway visited Canada in May 2002, they were entertained at a state dinner where the emphasis was on seasonal products that showcased many regions of the country. The appetizer was a salad of first-picked local fiddleheads, false morel mushrooms, baby leeks, and Atlantic lobster, served alongside a small fillet of pan-fried Lake Winnipeg pickerel. The main course included a venison medallion from northern Ontario, a loin of Quebec rabbit, and a white asparagus flan. After a selection of Canadian cheeses, the meal was completed with a fresh rhubarb crumble and a sorbet made of soy milk and Canadian wild ginger.

For Canadian guests invited to a function at Rideau Hall, a dish that reminds them of their own particular roots both acknowledges and honours them. For visitors from abroad, these menus project a very different image from the traditional idea of Canada and its heritage.

Adrienne Clarkson and John Ralston Saul share a laugh with young members of the Hutterite community of Baildon, Saskatchewan, in September 2001. AC: "When we were there we ate the most delicious chicken dumpling soup, but the cooks in the communal kitchen told us they wished we would come back to taste their Chinese food!"

PEI Potato Blini with Smoked Sturgeon, Fennel Crème Fraîche, and Caviar

The Rideau Hall chefs use sturgeon from the Pontiac region, which borders the Outaouais, and smoked at Boucanerie Chelsea, just north of Ottawa. The sturgeon caviar comes from Abitibi in northwestern Quebec—a source of fine caviar for fifty years. Blini are of East European origin, but instead of the usual flour and yeast, the chefs use PEI potatoes for starch.

To steam potatoes: when steamed, potatoes won't absorb as much water. Place a sieve over a pot of boiling water. Add the potatoes, cut in 1/2-inch cubes, and steam for 30 minutes or until a toothpick goes through with no resistance.

Suggested wine: Southbrook Farm Winery Sauvignon Blanc

Presentation

Place a few blini on each plate and garnish with a dab of crème fraîche, a slice of sturgeon, and a small spoonful of caviar. Decorate with a little fennel frond and serve.

Serves 4

for crème fraîche

2 cups (500 mL) heavy cream
1 tbsp (15 mL) buttermilk
1 tbsp (15 mL) freshly squeezed lemon juice
3 to 4 tbsp (45 mL to 60 mL) finely chopped fresh fennel fronds (the feathery tops of the fennel stalks)

for blini

2 PEI baking potatoes, peeled, diced, and steamed (see sidebar)
1 large egg
1 egg yolk
2 tbsp (30 mL) crème fraîche
2 tbsp (30 mL) all-purpose flour
pinch salt
2 tbsp (30 mL) chopped fresh dill
8 slices smoked sturgeon
1 ounce (28 g) sturgeon caviar

for crème fraîche

In a medium bowl, mix the cream, buttermilk, and lemon juice. Cover and leave in a warm spot for 24 hours; it should resemble sour cream. Mix the chopped fennel with the crème fraîche when you are ready to serve.

for blini

Place hot potatoes in a medium bowl and quickly mash until smooth. Add the crème fraîche.

In another bowl, mix the eggs, flour, and salt. Then blend into the potatoes until batter has thickened.

Preheat a griddle to 350°F (175°C) or a frying pan on medium heat and butter the surface. Spoon out or pipe loonie-sized circles of batter. Turn after 1 minute, and cook for 1 minute more. Each mini pancake should be golden brown and 1/4 inch thick when done.

Squash and Pemmican Flan with Three Sisters Salad in a Herb Sumac Vinaigrette

Flan, a firm custard, is not usually made from squash, one of the traditional "three sisters" of native North American agriculture, the others being corn and green beans.

You can incorporate pemmican into your daily cuisine by adding it to soup or a stir-fry, sprinkling it on a salad (instead of bacon bits), or rubbing it onto your steak before grilling. The Rideau Hall chefs use pemmican in various creative ways: as a dusting with herbs for fowl and monkfish, as part of a wild mushroom soufflé, and even in a cookie recipe.

Mary Richard's Pemmican Recipe
Smoke 5 lbs (2.25 kg) of beef or buffalo for 3 hours or until dry (this can be done in a small electric smoker). Dry 4 quarts (4 L) of saskatoon berries in an open oven on low heat for 48 hours. Wrap the meat in canvas and crush it with a mallet. Put the crushed meat in a blender, grind, and transfer it to a bowl. Add the dried saskatoon berries to the blender, grind, and remove. Mix equal portions of the meat to the berries.

Suggested wine: Nk'Mip Pinot Blanc

Serves 4

for flan

2 cups (500 mL) peeled and diced butternut squash
1/4 cup (62 mL) diced onion
1/2 clove garlic, chopped
1 cup (250 mL) heavy cream
2 egg yolks
1 tbsp (15 mL) pemmican (see sidebar)
pinch nutmeg
salt and pepper
1 tsp (5 mL) chopped fresh thyme
1 tbsp (15 mL) chopped flat-leaf parsley

for salad

1/4 lb (115 g) fine green beans, cut into 1-inch pieces
1 cup (250 mL) peeled and diced butternut squash
3 tbsp (45 mL) grapeseed oil
1 cup (250 mL) fresh cooked (or frozen) corn kernels
1/2 cup (125 mL) diced red onion
1 clove garlic, chopped
2 tbsp (30 mL) white balsamic vinegar or rice wine vinegar
2 tbsp (30 mL) chopped flat-leaf parsley
2 tbsp (30 mL) chopped fresh chives

for vinaigrette

1 tsp (5 mL) Dijon mustard
1 tbsp (15 mL) finely diced shallot
2 tbsp (30 mL) white balsamic vinegar or rice wine vinegar
3/4 cup (187 mL) canola oil
salt and cracked black peppercorns
1 tbsp (15 mL) ground sumac (available at Mediterranean or Middle Eastern food stores)
1/2 tsp (2 mL) chopped fresh tarragon
1/2 tsp (2 mL) chopped fresh thyme
1 tbsp (15 mL) chopped fresh chives
1 tbsp (15 mL) chopped flat-leaf parsley

Presentation

When the flan-filled ramekins have cooled, place one in the centre of each plate and serve with salad on the side. Drizzle the remaining vinaigrette over the entire dish, then sprinkle with the rest of the pemmican.

for flan

Butter the inside of four 4-ounce (120 mL) ramekins.

Cook the squash in boiling water for 5 minutes or until it is fork-tender. Set aside. Sauté the onion and garlic until the onion is translucent and the garlic is golden. Add the squash, season with salt and pepper, and sauté for another 30 seconds.

Transfer the mixture to a food processor and blend until smooth. Add the egg yolks and cream and blend well. Remove and pass the mixture through a sieve into a bowl. Fold in the remaining ingredients except for the pemmican.

Fill the ramekins with the flan mixture and sprinkle with half the pemmican. Bake at 350°F (180°C) in a bain-marie (a 2-inch-high baking pan containing 1 inch of water) for 40 minutes or until the flan is set like a custard, fully cooked yet still soft. Carefully remove the ramekins from the oven and cool at room temperature.

for salad

In a large pot of boiling salted water, cook the green beans for 6 to 7 minutes or until they are al dente. Remove immediately from the heat, drain, and place in an ice-water bath for 15 seconds. Drain and set aside.

Meanwhile, in a pot of boiling salted water, cook the squash for 2 minutes; drain, and place in an ovenproof dish. Toss with 1 tbsp grapeseed oil, season with salt and pepper, and bake in a 450°F–500°F (230°C–260°C) oven for 7 to 10 minutes or until nicely roasted. Remove from the heat and allow to cool.

In a very hot skillet, stir-fry the corn in 1 tbsp grapeseed oil until it is nicely browned. Add the onion and garlic and stir-fry the mixture for another minute. Deglaze the pan by adding vinegar and bringing it to a boil while scraping up the browned bits on the bottom. When the liquid is reduced, set it aside to cool. Once cooled, with the squash, beans, herbs, and remaining grapeseed oil in a large bowl.

for vinaigrette

Combine ingredients in a jar and shake vigorously for 30 seconds or until well-mixed. Toss salad with half the vinaigrette.

Barbecued Caribou Tenderloin with Grilled Vegetables in a Juniper Tea Vinaigrette

The preferred way to eat caribou in the Arctic is raw and frozen, sliced thin. But if you cook it on a spit over an open flame, as the chefs at Rideau Hall do, you get a smoky flavor.

Juniper tea is made from the juniper bushes harvested in Nunavik. For centuries the Inuit have made teas from local berries and herbs. Today, chefs across Canada use these teas in a variety of sauces, vinaigrettes, and desserts.

Suggested wine: Henry of Pelham Baco Noir Reserve

Presentation
Drizzle the vinaigrette over the grilled vegetables and serve with the caribou.

Serves 4

for tenderloin

1 lb (450 g) caribou tenderloin
kosher salt
1 tbsp (15 mL) maple syrup
1 tsp (5 mL) ground juniper berries
1 tsp (5 mL) cracked black peppercorns
1 tbsp (15 mL) red wine vinegar
1 tbsp (15 mL) finely chopped scallions
2 tbsp (30 mL) grapeseed oil

for grilled vegetables

2 eggplant round slices, each 1⁄2 inch (1.25 cm) thick
1 medium zucchini
1 medium carrot or 4 baby carrots with green tops
2 scallions
2 large radishes
1 tbsp (15 mL) grapeseed oil
salt and cracked black peppercorns

for vinaigrette

1 bag juniper tea or other herbal tea
1 1⁄2 tbsp (22 mL) red wine vinegar
1 tsp (5 mL) Dijon mustard
6 juniper berries, ground with mortar and pestle
1 tsp (5 mL) finely chopped shallot
2 tbsp (30 mL) grapeseed oil
1 tsp (5 mL) red berry coulis, purée, syrup, or jam (optional)
1 tsp (5 mL) chopped flat-leaf parsley
1 tsp (5 mL) chopped fresh thyme
salt and cracked black peppercorns

for tenderloin
Cut the tenderloin into 4-ounce (125 g) portions or ask your butcher to do it. Set aside.

In a small bowl, mix together the maple syrup, juniper berries, pepper, vinegar, scallions, and grapeseed oil. One hour before grilling, pour the marinade over the tenderloin pieces in a plastic bag, seal, and leave the bag at room temperature.

When ready to grill, remove the tenderloin pieces from the marinade and generously season them with salt on all sides. Over a very hot barbecue, grill the tenderloin 4 minutes for rare, 6 minutes for medium, turning every minute. Once they are done, set them aside.

for grilled vegetables
On a plate, arrange the two slices of eggplant, brush with a little oil, then sprinkle with salt. Leave them at room temperature for an hour, then cut both pieces in half and place them between two paper towels to absorb excess water, applying gentle pressure with your hand. Set aside.

Cut the zucchini in half, then cut each half lengthwise. Cut the radishes in half. Blanch both in boiling salted water for 15 seconds, remove, and place under cold running water. Set aside. Peel the carrot and cut it into sticks, ½-inch thick. Blanch in a pot of boiling salted water for 2 to 3 minutes or until tender. Set aside.

Cut the scallions diagonally into 1-inch pieces. Oil and season the vegetables and grill them over a barbecue on high for 3 to 4 minutes.

for vinaigrette
In a small cup, pour the vinegar over the tea bag and leave in a warm area for 10 minutes to infuse. Remove the tea bag, squeeze the excess vinegar back into the cup, and discard the bag.

In a small bowl, whisk together the infused vinegar, mustard, ground berries, and shallot (and red berry coulis). Add the grapeseed oil and continue whisking until the mixture is emulsified. Add the chopped thyme and parsley.

Maple Nut Bannock Bread

Scottish immigrants brought this flatbread recipe with them to Canada, inspired by traditional scones. Bannock became the perfect food for the First Nations people to bring along on hunting expeditions because it has few ingredients, can be cooked on an outdoor fire, and doesn't require the dough to rise. It can be made in many variations, merely by adding dry fruits or herbs to the flour-oil-water mixture.

The chefs of Rideau Hall bake variations of the traditional bannock bread to make melba toast to serve with cheeses or as interesting croutons for salads. Bannock bread is also used in savoury bread puddings, as a base for canapés, or as part of a terrine served at a buffet.

Makes 1 loaf

3 1/2 cups (875 mL) all-purpose flour
2 tsp (10 mL) salt
2 tbsp (30 mL) baking powder
1/2 tsp (2 mL) baking soda
1 cup (250 mL) chopped hazelnuts and walnuts
1 cup (250 mL) buttermilk
1 cup (250 mL) apple juice
3 tbsp (45 mL) maple syrup
1 1/2 tbsp (22 mL) melted shortening, butter, or margarine

Preheat the oven to 375°F (190°C). In a medium bowl, mix together the flour, salt, baking powder, baking soda, and nuts. In a separate bowl, mix together the buttermilk, apple juice, maple syrup, and shortening. Add the wet mixture to the dry and blend just enough so that the mixture is completely integrated. Be careful not to overmix.

Pour the mixture into an oiled 8-inch x 9-inch x 1/2-inch baking pan and bake for 30 to 35 minutes or until the top is golden brown and slightly cracked.

Maple Nut Bannock Bread Pudding with Saskatoon Berry Compote and Crème Anglaise

This basic bread pudding recipe can be adapted according to what is seasonally available. The chefs at Rideau Hall sometimes serve bread pudding topped with a compote made of saskatoon berries and bush cranberries flavoured with orange and lemon zest and spiced with cinnamon and ginger, then finish it off with a generous serving of crème anglaise. But you can create your own variation. Substitute any wild berry jam for the compote or try it with maple syrup. Instead of crème anglaise, you could top it with whipped cream or crème fraîche. Or you could simply serve it with a fruit sorbet or ice cream.

Suggested wine: Sumac Ridge Select Late Harvest Gewürztraminer

- 2 cups (500 mL) milk
- 4 large eggs
- 2 egg yolks
- ½ cup (125 mL) granulated sugar
- 1 tbsp (15 mL) vanilla extract or one vanilla bean, split and seeded
- ½ tsp (2 mL) ground nutmeg
- 1 ounce (30 mL) melted unsalted butter
- 2 cups (500 mL) cubed bannock bread (see previous page)

In a large bowl, mix together milk, eggs, egg yolks, sugar, vanilla, nutmeg, and butter until fully combined. Incorporate the cubed bannock bread into the mixture and set aside. Butter an 8-inch-by-8-inch (2 L) earthenware dish and fill with the pudding mixture. Refrigerate overnight.

About an hour before serving, preheat oven to 325°F (160°C). Place the earthenware dish containing the bread pudding mixture into a bain-marie (a 1-inch-deep water bath); put it in the oven and bake for 40 minutes or until a toothpick inserted in the middle comes out clean.

With a large spoon, portion the warm pudding onto plates; garnish with a spoonful of compote and a generous serving of crème anglaise over each serving.

CHAPTER 3

Showing Off Canadian Wine

Canadian wine, with its strong presence of fruit, has developed a unique cool-climate signature. It has established its place in the family of New World wines.

Riesling grape vine at Thirty Bench Winery near Beamsville in Ontario's Niagara Peninsula. Riesling is one of the most widely planted grape varieties in Canada and makes some of our finest wine.

A Completely Canadian Cellar

As recently as the late 1990s the wine cellar in Canada's House held few bottles of Canadian wines—it was stocked instead with wines imported from other countries, a situation ripe for change. John Ralston Saul was a passionate advocate for Canadian wine before he arrived at Rideau Hall with Adrienne Clarkson, so Canadianizing the wine cellar as a way to show off Canadian wine became an important goal. He found an enthusiastic ally in Pierre Laframboise, who had been hired to oversee the daily contracting services for all goods and supplies. Laframboise brought with him the experience of a twenty-year career in the restaurant and catering industry as well as a particular passion for Canadian wines. In a few short years the two have helped transform the wine cellar at Rideau Hall into a showcase for Canadian wines and winemakers.

Only recently have Canadian wines been recognized internationally as the product of an interesting and distinct cool climate wine region. Overall production may seem marginal compared to international standards (10,000 hectares of vines are cultivated in Canada, and 873,000 in France), but our wines have won numerous awards and distinctions in the past several years and have been praised by experts from around the world. And given the intensive pattern of new planting now underway there should be a total of 16,000 hectares in another decade.

Until the 1970s, Canada did not produce wine of international quality. We grew mainly labrusca vines, which produce a variety of grapes excellent for pies and jellies but unsuitable for winemaking. Remember those almost undrinkable sparkling rosés and sparkling burgundies? No wonder most European wine producers ridiculed Canadian wines.

Throughout the world, good table wines are made with grapes from vinifera vines, which bear grapes that have proven themselves in established wine-growing regions in Europe and elsewhere. Many of these varietals will be familiar—Riesling,

Chardonnay, Gewürztraminer, Sauvignon Blanc, Pinot Noir, Pinot Blanc, Pinot Gris, Cabernet Sauvignon, Merlot, Syrah—all of which come from vinifera clones. A clone results from an intense research process in which vine nurseries select the best characteristics from different vines and use them to improve the quality of the vines they sell.

As far back as the 1960s, some grape growers in Ontario and British Columbia were already planting these better-quality vinifera vines, but only in relatively small quantities. Things began to change, slowly, at the end of the 1970s, with the arrival on the scene of a handful of visionary winemakers, people like Joseph Zimmerman, who planted vinifera vines in the Okanagan for the Jordan & Ste-Michelle winery, or Don Ziraldo and Karl Kaiser of Inniskillin in Niagara-on-the-Lake. These pioneers were among the first to plant vinifera grapes. By the early 1980s they were proving that excellent wines could be produced both in British Columbia and in Ontario. Following their lead, other producers in our two primary wine-growing regions quickly began to replace all the old labrusca vines with clones of the vinifera varieties and to introduce modern winemaking techniques.

The wine that first brought Canada international recognition was icewine, which was pioneered by Inniskillin's Kaiser and Ziraldo. Icewine originated in cool climate regions like Germany and Austria. To make icewine, the grapes must not

Canadian Wines Come of Age

Canadians are making some of the best wine in the world and it's important to celebrate the fact. Our wines are more and more what wine experts call fruit-driven—because we have very good fruit on the vines, the winemakers don't have to chaptalize—add sugar—as is common in mid to northern Europe. And our climate runs from dry to mid-dry, a range that, combined with sun levels, means that, unlike in much of Europe, the winemakers don't have to use much sulphur. (Many people who say they are allergic to white wines are really reacting to the sulphur.) Because our wines are more natural and more stable, our winemakers need to add few chemicals. Ironically, the fruit is so good because, in both our major wine regions, the climate is marginal—conditions that cause the fruit taste to come forward. In places like California, where you can't taste the fruit, it's because there's so much sun, and therefore not enough acidity, and the wine is out of balance. Interestingly, this marginal climate links Niagara and the Okanagan with Burgundy. Some of the best Canadian Pinot Noirs and Chardonnays are on par with the best wines from Burgundy—and ours are a lot less expensive.

We are making very sophisticated wines—wines that let their natural fruit come through rather than masking their essential varietal character, wines that are allowed to taste like themselves. And the more naturally the grapes are grown, the better. All this requires great skill: it's easier to mask the ingredients than to try to work with their individual character. *JRS*

Vidal grapes left well past the first frost await harvest for icewine. To meet VQA standards—the most rigorous in the world—the grapes must be naturally, not artificially frozen. This means the winemaker has a very small window of opportunity—usually late at night starting around 3 am. The grapes must be handpicked and must stay frozen during the complete picking and crushing process. If the temperature does not drop enough, the grapes are reclassified for late-harvest wine.

GOLD MEDAL WINNER
SILVER MEDAL WINNER
GOLD MEDAL WINNER

Given the excellence of Canadian wines, why shouldn't Rideau Hall have Canada's greatest wine cellar, a cellar made up entirely of Canadian wines? It's a smart way to show off Canadian excellence to the world.

JOHN RALSTON SAUL

be picked until after they have frozen on the vines. They are harvested by hand at temperatures between −10° and −13°C. When these frozen grapes are pressed, they yield a few precious drops of very sweet and syrupy juice, which is high in sugar and rich in acidity and intense fruit flavours. Because Niagara has much in common with the icewine regions of Germany and Austria, Kaiser and Ziraldo believed they could make a great one. They were right. Today, Canada is the world's largest producer of icewine.

By the early 1980s, many other Canadian wines were beginning to show signs of excellence. An important indication that the industry was maturing came with the establishment of the quality-control appellation VQA (Vintners Quality Alliance). Adopted in 1988 in Ontario and in 1990 in British Columbia, VQA guarantees high standards for every wine that bears its imprimatur. It also defines the geographic limits of each wine-growing region and determines what types of grapes can be grown and the methods that can be used in wine production. And before a wine is allowed to display a VQA logo, it has to be approved by a wine-tasting committee.

The arrival of a second generation of Canadian vintners—many of them the sons and daughters of the first wave of serious Canadian growers and producers—coincided with a fundamental economic change: the 1989 Free Trade Agreement between Canada and the United States, which phased in an open market for North American wine. The new generation of Canadian winemakers immediately realized that they would have to adapt if they wanted to compete at home and abroad. They understood that success in Canada and in export markets depended on shifting rapidly to high-quality niche products.

They decided to position Canada as a cool climate region producing unique red and white wines with an obvious fruity note and subtle woody flavours, alongside the fine icewines and late-harvest wines that were winning international recognition year after year. At the same time, they continued to work at developing the ideal vinifera vines for our latitude and microclimates.

A bottling line at Henry of Pelham Winery near St. Catharines, Ontario. Ontario's total VQA wine production in 2002–2003 was almost 12 million litres, with sixty-six wineries belonging to the Vintners Quality Alliance.

The challenge now was to make the best wine possible. To this end, these young entrepreneurs recruited experienced winemakers from Europe, Australia, New Zealand, South Africa, and the United States; they invested in state-of-the-art viticulture equipment; they promoted exchanges with major producers in Europe and the United States to increase their expertise; and they put money into research and development, including the creation of wine institutes in Ontario and British Columbia dedicated to research and training in cool climate winemaking. As a result of all these efforts, Canadian vintners have become some of the world's leading experts on cool climate winemaking.

Above: A cellar for barrel-aging red wines before they are bottled at Hillebrand Winery near Virgil, Ontario. Canada is now starting to produce its own oak barrels rather than importing them from Europe or the United States. *Opposite*: Bottles of Hillebrand's Champagne-style sparkling wine aging on its lees.

Canadians are already drinking the results of these reforms. This country may not produce much wine, but it does produce very good wine. Our reds, whites, and sparkling wines are also now acclaimed international award winners. Year after year they score highly in important competitions such as VinItaly, Vinexpo de Bordeaux, Chardonnay du Monde, Riesling du Monde, Challenge International du Vin, and the International Wine and Spirits Competition.

Thirty years ago, not many Canadians were drinking wine. Thanks to a blossoming interest in food and travel, however, more and more people have become knowledgeable about wine, creating a domestic market. But we still have a long way to go. According to statistics from the Canadian Vintners Association, between 1995 and 2002 sales of VQA wines tripled from 3,157,641 litres to 9,583,380 litres. Yet Agriculture Canada's statistics show that the Canadian wines account for less than 40 percent of wine sold in Canada. By comparison, the United States, France, Australia, and Italy each control about 85 percent of its national market.

A considerable part of the problem, however, lies in the inadequate domestic distribution system. Provincial liquor corporations, most of which operate a distribution monopoly, have been slow to stock domestic wines. In Quebec, for instance, it is still almost impossible to find a wine from British Columbia and very difficult to find Ontario wines, while a huge selection of Chilean or California wines is available.

Canada's Wine Regions

Our two main wine-producing regions, Niagara in Ontario and the Okanagan Valley in British Columbia, are both crafting wines of the highest quality that compare favourably with wines being made anywhere in the world, and winning many international awards. And the Rideau Hall wine cellar is now a 100 percent Canadian cellar, one that is well on its way to becoming the finest of its kind and an extraordinary showcase for the Canadian wine industry. It normally contains about 4,000 bottles of VQA wines from Ontario and British Columbia, the only two provinces with officially designated viticultural areas, a selection that represents a wide variety of wineries and many different styles. The very high quality of this cellar is an indicator of just how good Canadian wines have become.

In order to raise the profile of Canadian wine, Saul and Laframboise organize visits each year to the Okanagan and to Niagara, inviting foreign diplomats, who taste the newest vintages, learn about cool climate winemaking, and discover Canada's unique wine-making *savoir faire*.

British Columbia

The story of British Columbia wine is really the story of the Okanagan Valley, which produces 95 percent of the province's wine. It isn't hard to imagine why the first settlers chose to stop when they reached this valley. Visitors cannot help but be impressed each time they drive over the crest of the low mountains capped by rocky, forested promontories. Below the crest, the steep slopes are covered with symmetrical rows of vines and fruit trees, which, on a still, windless day, are reflected in the mirrorlike lake.

Climate, terrain, and soil type determine a region's wine growing characteristics and its unique terroir, and the 180-kilometre-long Okanagan Valley is blessed, protected by the Rocky Mountains to the east and the coastal chain to the west, which creates an almost ideal microclimate for growing the winemaking grapes. The protection provided by the surrounding mountains, combined with the breeze coming from

A view south over a vineyard of Pinot Blanc, looking towards McIntyre Bluff in British Columbia's Okanagan Valley. The Okanagan is one of Canada's two primary wine-growing areas and accounts for the bulk of wine made west of the Rockies. In British Columbia, total VQA wine production in 2002, exceeded 4 million litres, and forty-nine wineries were members of the British Columbia Wine Institute, which administers the VQA program in that province.

the lake, causes what's known as an inversion factor: while the mountains keep the warm air from moving on, the lake in summer has a cooling effect that protects the vines from too much heat, and in winter has a warming effect, reducing the risk of frost. The soil of the valley is renowned for its fertility, making it one of the best horticultural regions in the country, if not the world.

There are important climatic and geological differences between the north and the south of the valley. In the south, from Oliver to Osoyoos, the soil is a mixture of sand and gravel, and, with less than 15 millimetres of rainfall annually, it is the only true desert in Canada (apart from much of the Arctic). Near the American border, the part of the valley where viticulture is still quite new, red wines dominate. In this desert area, BC wineries have planted vineyards made up largely of Merlot, Cabernet Sauvignon, and Pinot Noir. John Ralston Saul and Pierre Laframboise were impressed with the production of Pinot Noir and Merlot at Nk'Mip Cellars when they visited the winery in Osoyoos in 2003. Nk'Mip is the only North American winery owned by a First Nations band, a partnership between Vincor International and the Osoyoos Band Council.

In nearby Oliver, Vincor, which is Canada's largest wine company, is also involved in another interesting partnership with Château Gruaud Larose of Bordeaux, France. The Osoyoos Larose Winery has created a Bordeaux-style wine that sets a new standard in Canadian wines. The desert-like conditions along with an ideal soil and the full sun exposure of the southern Okanagan have allowed a number of fine vineyards to flourish. This group includes Tinhorn Creek, known for its high-quality Merlots and Cabernets; Burrowing Owl, which makes fine Cabernet Francs and Syrahs; and Domaine de Combret, which has won honours for its Gamays.

The northern part of the valley receives only about 40 centimetres of rain annually, most of it in the winter months. Because of the dryness of the Okanagan's summer climate, its vineyards can survive and thrive only with regular irrigation.

Opposite top: Ripe Riesling grapes. *Opposite below*: Pinot Noir grapes ready for harvest. JRS: "My own feeling is that Canada is now among the two or three best producers in the world of Rieslings, whether dry or sweet. And while our production of Pinot Noir is still relatively small, we already seem to be one of a handful of countries outside of France that produce first-class wine from this most difficult of grapes. We also seem to be naturals at making sparkling wine. At blind tastings, Canadian sparkling wines defeat sparkling wines and Champagnes from all over the world."

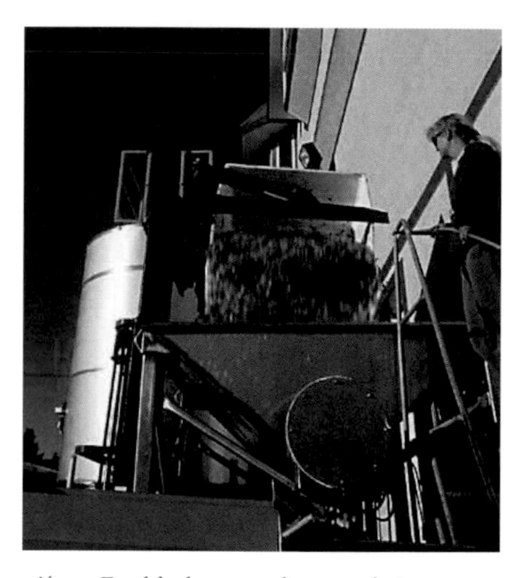

Above: Freshly harvested grapes being delivered to a crusher, where their juice will be extracted. *Opposite*: The dramatic setting of BC's Mission Hill Estate Winery.

But these dry growing conditions provide an important advantage for vintners: vines are less prone to disease than in other cool climate regions, such as the Burgundy region of France.

The division between the north and the south of the Okanagan is blurred. Some of the valley's best Pinot Noir is grown in the north near Kelowna, at Quails' Gate Winery, which also produces an excellent Maréchal Foch, a vigorous red made of French hybrid grapes. The wine comes from very old vines, which generally yield fewer grapes, but of higher quality, that produce wines rich in fruit flavours and intense aromas—making them ideal for food pairing.

Quails' Gate has distinguished itself in recent years, winning many international prizes, notably for its Rieslings and Chardonnays, so it has become a regular stop during Rideau Hall's working visits. So has the family estate Cedar Creek, located directly across the lake. Family estates are medium-sized wineries producing between 30,000 and 60,000 cases of wine each year. Cedar Creek has found its niche producing fine Pinot Blanc and Pinot Noir, along with Meritage Bordeaux-type wines.

Another important stop is the 750-metre summit of Mount Boucherie, the site of British Columbia's largest independent winery, Mission Hill. The location is magnificent, filled with rose gardens and overlooking the northern part of Lake Okanagan. A twelve-storey bell tower dominates the striking cathedral-like structure of the Mission Hill Winery, yet the architecture remains secondary to the extraordinary scenery of the valley. This European-style winery was founded in 1981 by a young visionary, Anthony von Mandl. It produces 140,000 cases of wine annually and draws more than 150,000 visitors each year. Mission Hill owns vineyards throughout the Okanagan, as do the other major players, enabling it to create a wide variety of superior-quality wines: Pinot Blanc, Pinot Gris, Riesling, Cabernet Sauvignon, Pinot Noir, and Shiraz.

Sumac Ridge, British Columbia's first estate winery, is in nearby Summerland. It was founded in 1979 by Harry

McWatters, who continues to oversee production and has made it into an award-winning winery. It too is now owned by Vincor International.

In all, about fifty wineries line the slopes of the Okanagan Valley. The wine they make is already very good—and it will continue to get better.

Ontario

As with the Okanagan, what makes Niagara so special for growing grapes and making wine is its particular combination of soil and microclimate. The soil is, for the most part, a mix of glacial till—rich in sediments and clay loam deposited by glacial rivers and lakes—which makes for excellent drainage and causes the roots of the vines to search deep for nutrients. In summer the vineyards benefit from the onshore breezes, which are then buffeted back to the lake and help to maintain a continuous airflow, while from January to March, cold air is kept in the upper altitudes, reducing the risk of severe ground frosts. A ledge known as the Bench, which runs parallel to the Niagara Escarpment, receives the full benefit of this unique microclimate. It is here that most of the region's best wine grapes are grown.

The Niagara Peninsula is often compared to the Burgundy region of France, the birthplace of two of the world's most famous wine grapes: Chardonnay and Pinot Noir. Chardonnay is now the world's most popular wine and, in the last twenty-five years, has become Niagara's most widely planted variety. Pinot Noir is an unpredictable variety that can produce marvels in the hands of experts. The vines cultivated in cooler climates are renowned for producing wines with a strong fruity presence and with aromas more concentrated than those coming from warmer regions.

And just as winemakers from the Okanagan now look forward each year to the annual Rideau Hall visit, so do their colleagues from Niagara. The visit always coincides with Niagara's famous Cuvée, always on the first weekend of March, an event that celebrates the region's best wineries with guided tastings and special tours. Cuvée is a wonderful

From an overlook high on the Niagara Escarpment near Beamsville, Ontario, the view sweeps down over Cave Spring's vineyards to Lake Ontario and the Toronto skyline in the distance. The lake and escarpment combine to create the favourable microclimate in which wine grapes can flourish.

way to introduce and promote Canadian wines to thousands of visitors.

Most of Niagara's fifty or so VQA wineries are family estates. Some of the more familiar names include Cave Spring, Henry of Pelham, Peninsula Ridge, Daniel Lenko, Château des Charmes, Vineland Estates, and Lailey. They flourish alongside some very big players, like Andres Wines, which owns Peller and Hillebrand, and Vincor International, the owner of Inniskillin and Jackson-Triggs.

Cave Spring Cellars, based in the village of Jordan, is one of the region's more established and well-respected wineries, producing 60,000 cases annually. Owner Len Pennachetti and

winemaker Angelo Pavan have been producing quality wines since 1986: Gewürztraminer, an award-winning Riesling, Chardonnay, Gamay, and some exceptional Chenin Blanc, which are made from some of the oldest vinifera vines in Ontario. Peninsula Ridge is a new winery that sought out the expertise of French winemaker and Chablis specialist Jean-Pierre Colas, and it is already producing an exceptional Sauvignon Blanc.

Ontario has long been recognized for its white wines, but is now creating reds typical of its northern terroir. The Speck brothers of Henry of Pelham in St. Catharines are known for their Baco Noir, a hybrid that produces a wine with complex aromas, while their Merlot and sparkling rosé are also making waves. Don Triggs, the president of Vincor International, has formed a partnership with Boisset, the largest producer in Burgundy, to launch Le Clos Jordan, which will concentrate on high-quality Pinot Noir and Chardonnay. The Delaine vineyard, owned by Triggs and his wife, Elaine, is dedicated to seeking out quality clones while supplying vinifera grapes to the new Jackson-Triggs winery, whose state-of-the-art 4,200-square-metre installation is a tribute to modern viticulture and to Ontario agriculture. Finally, at Château des Charmes another pioneer, Paul-Michel Bosc, and his sons have spent countless hours researching clones that are well adapted to their specific terroir. They have already obtained some really promising results with different types of Gamays.

Building a Canadian Cellar

Clearly, Canada's two major wine regions provide more than enough variety to stock a wine cellar, but creating one from scratch doesn't take place overnight. What's been accomplished at Rideau Hall is a case study in how to build a great Canadian cellar. While many wines are made to be drunk young, others will only improve with age. Yet many of the best Canadian wines are released soon after bottling because the demand is high and the production is limited. Creating a cellar means buying both for the present and for the future—and that means making sure that wines are stored properly for

The Rideau Hall wine cellar may be housed in an ordinary basement storeroom, but it already sets the standard for a Canadian cellar. It is stocked from VQA producers in both of Canada's wine-growing regions as the result of blind and other comparative tastings, drawing from small farm wineries, estate wineries, and big producers.

aging. According to Laframboise, a few simple rules apply. Choose a quiet, clean room. Store the bottle lying flat so the cork will stay wet; a wet cork prevents air from getting in contact with the wine and causing it to spoil. Keep the room dark and maintain a steady temperature of between 12 and 14 degrees Celsius, with a humidity level of at least 40 percent. Professionals sometimes keep the humidity level of their wine cellars as high as 75 percent as a way to prevent the corks from drying out.

Laframboise keeps the humidity level in Rideau Hall's wine cellar at between 65 and 75 percent. The temperature is controlled electronically at 15 degrees Celsius. The cellar itself is utilitarian—a storage room of about 15 square metres in the basement of Rideau Hall, just a few steps from the kitchens. From the start, every year they laid down several wines with excellent potential for aging. These wines will be enjoyed at their peak by future visitors.

Grape vines about to flower on the Niagara Peninsula. Although a young vine begins to yield good fruit three years after planting, older vines will bear better-quality grapes. The trade-off is often quantity over quality. Old vines—twenty years and older—will bear fewer grapes but with more concentrated fruit that can lead to exceptional wine.

Pairing Wine and Food

Choosing a wine that will complement a particular dish is not as complicated as people generally think. Canadian VQA wines are especially easy to match because of their fine and delicate fruit.

There are a few basic rules to keep in mind. Light wines should be served with delicate dishes, whereas stronger flavours will require full-bodied wines. For a menu involving several courses, younger wines should be served first, since they are usually lighter. Once the menu has been created, choose a wine that can stand up to the boldest flavour on the plate, whether that's the meat, the vegetable, or the sauce. Spicy dishes usually go well with wines that have a residual sweetness, such as an off-dry Riesling, whereas smoky, salty, or oily dishes pair especially well with an acidic wine like a Chardonnay or a dry Riesling. Dessert wines should always be sweeter than the dish you are serving. And the serving temperature must be perfect if you are to taste the wine to its fullest: 8 to 9 degrees Celsius for most whites, 16 to 18 degrees for red wines like Pinot and Bordeaux, and 6 degrees for icewine.

A mélange of corks from top Canadian wineries. The biggest debate in the wine world these days is not about vintages or viticultural practices, but about cork versus plastic. More and more winemakers in Canada and elsewhere are using synthetic corks to preserve wine quality and prevent oxidation. (Roughly 10 percent of the bottles with natural corks acquire a corky taste that makes the wine all but undrinkable.)

Excellence Abroad

Canadian wine, with its strong presence of fruit, has developed a unique cool climate signature. It has established its place in the family of New World wines alongside California, Australia, New Zealand, Chile, and Argentina. Even in Old World countries, Canadian wines are making inroads.

A few years ago Canadian Riesling producers took part in a state visit to Germany. The result was a commercial agreement for the import of Canadian Rieslings to Germany, birthplace of the Riesling grape. During the 2004 state visit to Finland, a Canadian winery entered a blind tasting of seven Pinot Noirs from around the world held by the Association of Finnish Sommeliers (the people who choose the wines served in hotels and restaurants). The jury unanimously placed the Canadian wine, a 2001 Pinot Noir Family Reserve from Quails' Gate Winery in British Columbia, at the top. At several such events in Finland, and later in Iceland, our Scandinavian hosts concluded that Canada's cool climate wines were a natural match for their cool climate cuisine. As a result, Canadian vintners have opened up a new export market and signed contracts with the state liquor corporations in both countries.

As little as fifteen years ago, few would have predicted that Canadian wines would be served at a state dinner in Europe. Yet that was the case at the state dinners hosted by Finland and Iceland in 2003. No one is complaining that Canada's wines are now the only wines served at Canada's House. Our wines have truly come of age.

Layered Tomato and Feta Cheese with Ice Plant and Arugula Salad

When the Rideau Hall chefs use green, yellow, or red tomatoes, they tend to choose a heritage kind, but vine-ripened tomatoes will do just fine for this salad. Goat milk produces a variety of cheeses, each with a unique personality and a pungent flavour. David Wood, a farmer on Saltspring Island, BC, makes top-quality goat and sheep cheese. His Saint Joe feta goes particularly well in this salad dish. The ice plant is a firm, crunchy green that the Rideau Hall chefs buy from Fines herbes par Daniel. It has an interesting icy/crunchy texture, from which it gets its name. You can substitute any green sprout or even baby spinach.

Suggested wine: Henry of Pelham Sauvignon Blanc

Presentation
When ready to serve, alternate overlapping slices of tomatoes and feta cheese on each plate. Sprinkle with balsamic vinaigrette and top with a bouquet of lightly dressed salad. Spoon the infusion around the plate, add cracked black pepper, garnish with basil, and serve.

Serves 4

for infusion (to be made a day ahead)

1 clove garlic
3 tbsp (45 mL) chopped fresh basil
3 tbsp (45 mL) chopped fresh chives
3 scallions, green part only, sliced
3 tbsp (45 mL) extra-virgin olive oil

for salads

2 firm green tomatoes
2 firm yellow tomatoes
2 firm red tomatoes
1/2 lb (225 g) feta cheese
3 tbsp (45 mL) extra-virgin olive oil
2 tbsp (30 mL) chopped fresh basil
2 tbsp (30 mL) white balsamic vinegar or regular balsamic
cracked black peppercorns
kosher salt
1/4 cup (62 mL) ice plant or baby spinach
1/4 cup (62 mL) arugula
1 tbsp (15 mL) white balsamic vinegar or regular balsamic
2 tbsp (30 mL) extra-virgin olive oil

In a blender, pulse together the garlic, basil, chives, and scallions in a blender while slowly pouring in the olive oil until well mixed; then pour into a bowl, cover, and refrigerate overnight.

Slice the tomatoes 1/4 inch (6 mm) thick and set aside. Thinly slice the feta cheese to approximately half the thickness of the tomato slices. Mix the olive oil, basil, balsamic vinegar, and seasonings, then remove enough to dress the salad. Marinate the feta cheese in the remaining vinaigrette for a minimum of 30 minutes.

Herb-Marinated and Grilled Alberta Innisfail Lamb Chop

served with King Eringi Mushroom, Prairie Grain, and Leek Pilaf and Roasted Carrot, Red Turnip and Golden Beet

Any fresh Canadian lamb is right for this dish, but it seems especially right to use Alberta lamb in a menu that also calls for prairie grains. The chefs cook some of the grains and toast others to add a textural difference to this pilaf—or any other dish. When it comes to root vegetables, they often choose organically grown Cookstown Greens vegetables or vegetables from their own organic garden because they come in a wide variety of shapes and colours.

You will need to marinate the lamb chops for at least two hours before serving.

Suggested wine: Jackson-Triggs Okanagan Proprietor Reserve Meritage

Serves 4

for marinade

1 1/4 cup (310 mL) extra-virgin olive oil
3 cloves garlic, peeled and crushed
2 sprigs fresh rosemary
3 sprigs fresh thyme
1 tbsp (15 mL) cracked black peppercorns
8 small lamb chops or 4 large lamb chops
kosher salt and pepper

for pilaf

1/4 cup (62 mL) quinoa
1/3 cup (83 mL) millet
2 tbsp (30 mL) extra-virgin olive oil
1 leek, white part only, diced
5 ounces (140 g) eringi mushrooms, sliced
3 cloves garlic, chopped
salt and pepper
2 tbsp (30 mL) chopped flat-leaf parsley
1/4 cup (62 mL) diced shallots
2 tbsp (30 mL) chopped fresh chives

for vegetables

1 medium red carrot (or regular carrot)
1 medium yellow carrot (or regular carrot)
1 medium red turnip
1 medium golden beet
1/2 vidalia onion
3 tbsp (45 mL) chopped fresh chives
2 tbsp (30 mL) grapeseed oil
salt and pepper

for aioli
- 1⁄2 cup (125 mL) red wine
- 3 cloves garlic, finely chopped
- salt and pepper
- 1 egg yolk
- 3⁄4 cup (187 mL) extra-virgin olive oil
- 1 tbsp (15 mL) finely chopped fresh rosemary
- 1 tbsp (15 mL) red wine vinegar

for marinade

In a medium bowl, mix together the oil, garlic, rosemary, thyme, and pepper. Place the lamb chops in a tightly fitting container, pour marinade over them, and marinate for at least 1 to 2 hours. An hour before serving, remove the container from the refrigerator so that the lamb is at room temperature before grilling.

Preheat a stovetop grill or set the barbecue on medium-high heat. Remove the lamb from the marinade and salt the chops on all sides. Grill the chops to the desired doneness, turning every minute to allow the juices to distribute evenly. Once done, remove the chops from the heat and set them aside on a plate for at least 5 minutes.

for pilaf

Rinse the quinoa for several minutes under running water. Stir into 3⁄4 cup (175 mL) of salted boiling water. Cover and simmer for 15 minutes or until the water is absorbed and the grains are transparent.

Preheat the oven to 300°F (150°C). Rinse the millet under running water and drain. Transfer to a lightly oiled baking sheet and toast for 10 to 15 minutes or until lightly browned.

Meanwhile, in a large pan sauté the leek, garlic, and mushroom mixture in olive oil for 3 minutes or until the leeks are soft and the garlic is translucent. Season with salt and pepper, add the herbs, then mix in the millet and quinoa. Stir over medium heat for 2 more minutes. Serve hot with the lamb chops and roasted vegetables.

There are a number of ways to prepare aioli. If you prefer, substitute for the oil and egg yolk with 1 1⁄4 cup (300 mL) mayonnaise. Add the rest of the ingredients and prepare according to the instructions.

Presentation

Arrange the lamb, roasted vegetables, and pilaf on four plates, finishing with the aioli. (For additional flavour, drizzle the cooking juices from the resting platter into the aioli and mix.)

for vegetables

Preheat the oven to 500°F (260°C). Meanwhile, clean the vegetables and chop them to uniform size, approximately 2 inches in length.

In a large pot of boiling salted water, add the vegetables and cook them until just tender. Drain them and place in a roasting pan. Add oil, salt, and pepper; mix well.

Roast the vegetables for approximately 10 minutes or until they appear to caramelize. Remove from the oven and keep warm until you are ready to serve.

for aioli

In a stainless steel or copper pot over medium heat, add the red wine and simmer for 5 to 10 minutes or until reduced to approximately 1 tbsp (15 mL) and a syrupy consistency. Remove from the heat and set aside.

Place the garlic, salt, pepper, and yolk in a small bowl. Whisk in the oil slowly until it is fully incorporated. Add the rosemary, vinegar, and wine reduction. Adjust the seasoning to taste and set the aioli aside until you are ready to serve.

Fresh Ontario Goat Cheese Scone

Most provinces in the country produce very fine goat cheese: New Brunswick, Quebec, Ontario, Alberta, and British Columbia have developed an expertise and an incredible variety of goat and sheep cheeses. For this scone, the Rideau Hall chefs choose a mild and creamy cheese that complements the Rideau Hall jams.

Rideau Hall serves scones every Remembrance Day for the Silver Cross Mothers' tea—an event for veterans held at Rideau Hall following the memorial service at the National War Memorial. The Silver Cross—or Memorial Cross—was first awarded in 1919 to mothers and widows of Canadian soldiers who had died on active duty.

Serves 4

- 1 cup (250 mL) plus 1 tbsp (15 mL) all-purpose flour
- 1/2 tbsp (7 mL) baking powder
- 1/2 tsp (2 mL) salt
- zest of half a lemon
- 1 tbsp (15 mL) finely chopped fresh thyme
- 1/3 cup (83 mL) coarsely chopped cold unsalted butter
- 1/3 cup (83 mL) crumbled cold fresh goat cheese
- 1/4 cup (62 mL) heavy cream
- 1 tbsp (15 mL) fresh lemon juice
- 1 large egg
- 1 egg yolk
- 1 tbsp (15 mL) milk
- pinch salt

Sift the flour, baking powder, and salt into a large bowl. Add the lemon zest and thyme to the flour mixture. Coarsely grate the cold butter into the mixture. Add the crumbled goat cheese and, using your hands, mix the butter and cheese into a coarse meal.

In a separate bowl, mix together the cream, lemon juice, and egg. Add to the flour-butter mixture and blend just until the dough has come together and the flour is incorporated. Refrigerate for about 10 minutes to allow the gluten in the flour to relax.

On a lightly floured surface, roll out the dough to a 1/2-inch (1.25 cm) thickness. Using a 2-inch (5 cm) round cookie cutter, quickly and cleanly cut out each scone. Push the cutter straight down through the dough so that the sides of the dough are not "pinched." Place the scones on a parchment-lined baking sheet. Mix the egg yolk, milk, and a pinch of salt and brush a little onto the top of each scone.

Bake in a preheated 375°F (190°C) oven for about 15 minutes or until the tops of the scones are a golden brown. Serve warm.

Niagara Walnut and Maple Sugar Pie

The early settlers of Nouvelle-France learned to harvest maple sap and to boil it to make syrup and other delights, including a pie made with maple sugar. This is the Rideau Hall variation on traditional maple sugar pie—a great treat in the winter.

Suggested wine: Cave Spring Cellars Indian Summer Late Harvest Riesling

Makes one 9-inch (23 cm) pie

for crust

1 1/2 cups (375 mL) all-purpose flour
1/2 cup (125 mL) cold unsalted butter, cut into pieces
1/4 cup (62 mL) ice water

for filling

5 large eggs
1 cup (250 mL) packed brown sugar
3/4 cup (187 mL) maple syrup
1/2 cup (125 mL) corn syrup
3 tbsp (45 mL) melted unsalted butter
1 1/2 cups (375 mL) coarsely chopped walnuts

for crust

Lightly grease a 9-inch (23 cm) pie pan.

Using a stand mixer, preferably with a paddle attachment, mix the flour, butter, and water until a ball forms. (Depending on the quality of the ingredients or the time of year, more flour may be needed.) Wrap the dough in plastic and refrigerate for 15 minutes.

On a lightly floured surface, roll the dough into a 13-inch (33 cm) round, approximately 3/16 of an inch (5 mm) thick. Line the pie pan with the dough. Cut off any excess dough and crimp around the edges. Refrigerate the pie shell for at least 1 hour.

for filling

In a large mixing bowl, whisk the eggs and brown sugar until smooth. Add the maple syrup, corn syrup, and butter and continue stirring. To ensure that there are no lumps, strain the mixture through a wire sieve and set aside.

Preheat the oven to 325°F (160°C). Cover the inside of the pie shell with coarsely chopped walnuts. Slowly pour the filling over the walnuts. Place the pie in the oven and bake for 1 hour. Remove the pie from the oven and allow it to cool before slicing.

CHAPTER 4

Creating Canadian Menus The same careful planning goes into every meal served at the nation's table, whether it's a breakfast for a handful of special visitors or a luncheon for a newly accredited ambassador or a state dinner.

The copper pots in the kitchen have been at Rideau Hall for at least sixty years—probably longer. The biggest ones are very rare, being lined in traditional tin. *From top to bottom shelf*: 20-litre copper pots and large stainless-steel frying pans; 9-litre stainless-steel pots; 24-litre copper pots.

The creation of menus for official events at Rideau Hall demands careful coordination among all members of the Events Planning and Implementation team, led by Christine MacIntyre. Once the theme for an event has been established, executive chef Oliver Bartsch and executive sous-chef Louis Charest set about building a menu. Their brainstorming session usually takes place in Bartsch's tiny office in a corner of the kitchen. As often as possible, the dishes they choose reflect the seasonal availability of products. If root vegetables like celeriac and golden beets are ready to be harvested from the Rideau Hall gardens, the chefs may look to combine them with duck from Mariposa Farms in Ontario, a meat dish that can handle their intense flavours. Always they aim to bring together as many ingredients as possible from many different parts of Canada while maintaining a balance of tastes, colours, and textures on the plate. What's more, the menus are always one of a kind. The chefs pride themselves in never repeating a recipe for a public function—and that means creating hundreds of unique dishes every year. Simply browsing through a medley of appetizers is a little like taking a gastronomic tour of the whole country, as well as being a striking testimonial to the chefs' creativity: Nova Scotia Dragon's Breath Blue Cheese and Mariposa Farms Duck Confit Perogy; Licorice-Flavoured Quebec Foie Gras and Squash Pot Sticker; Jerk-Flavoured Quail Breast with a Cilantro and Fruit Salsa; Candied Niagara Plum Fried Wonton on a Caramel-Toasted Soy Bean Stick; Thai Arctic Shrimp on a Lemon Grass Skewer; Haida Gwaii Crab and Fried Oolichan Sushi Roll.

Once the chefs have drawn up a menu, wines are chosen to suit, and the kitchen brigade gets busy preparing whatever can be made in advance. It is not unusual for the staff to be working on several different events at once, for Rideau Hall often hosts two or three functions in one day. It might include an intimate breakfast with the prime minister and a few invited guests, a special luncheon in honour of a visiting dignitary, and a cocktail reception for Nordic ambassadors. So, while one chef may be chopping fresh mint to sprinkle on a dessert about to be served, another may be mixing a marinade for a piece of venison on a menu scheduled for a day or more later.

Bartsch and Charest work hard to make every menu suit the occasion. For the dinner following the Order of Canada ceremony in February 2003, they wanted to create a meal that mirrored the diverse origins of those being honoured with the country's highest civil distinction—people who came from across the country. And so did the food.

The evening began with a glass of classic Inniskillin Klose Vineyard Chardonnay from the Niagara region of Ontario served with several inventive hors d'oeuvre: traditional ravioli stuffed with foie gras butter from Quebec and crab from Nova Scotia; grilled bannock bread topped with Arctic char tartare garnished with daisy capers; tiny puff pastries made with Leoni-Grana, a Parmesan-style cheese from Alberta, and accompanied by a sweetbread ragout and pancetta. Even before the guests sat down for dinner, they had sampled food that reflected several parts of the country. And this was only a foretaste.

Once the diners were seated in the Rideau Hall Ballroom, beneath its huge glass chandelier and overlooked by the massive, tongue-in-cheek painting of Queen Elizabeth and Prince Philip by Jean-Paul Lemieux, they were served an appetizer that was a virtual microcosm of the country: Newfoundland and Labrador cod tongue and cod cheek on a citrus cake made with Nova Scotia sea parsley (a red seaweed rich in omega-3), next to a small fillet of pan-fried smoked black cod from British Columbia. This was accompanied by a salad of prairie grains and Ontario organic vegetables, and the whole dish was garnished with a tricoloured cracker made from a selection of organic flours from Quebec.

The main course turned into a pan-Canadian celebration: Manitoba bison tenderloin, served alongside rabbit loin from Saint-Apollinaire, a wild rice risotto and dried berry croquette, a braised red onion with caramelized squash purée, and parsnip chips sprinkled with a huckleberry bison reduction. To accompany the main course, a Tinhorn Creek Cabernet Franc from the Okanagan Valley was chosen, a

Detail of an Order of Canada dessert plate. The plates were commissioned during Governor General Léger's mandate to commemorate the tenth anniversary of the creation of the Order and were made by Royal Worcester Spode (Canada) Ltd. They are used only for Order of Canada dinners.

PATRIAM

wine robust enough to stand up to the gamey taste of Manitoba bison.

Between the main course and dessert, diners could taste a selection of five Canadian cheeses: Comox Camembert, a soft creamy cheese produced in Courtenay, BC (on the east coast of Vancouver Island); ash-ripened St. Maure, a semi-soft goat cheese produced in Ponoka, Alberta; C'est Bon goat cheese, a soft, unripened fresh cheese produced in St. Mary's, Ontario; Ciel de Charlevoix, a creamy blue cheese from Baie St-Paul, Quebec; and Le Gamin, a soft, washed-rind raw milk cheese from Sainte-Marie de Kent, New Brunswick. Many of the guests said they had no idea that Canada produced such superb cheeses.

The meal finished with a mousseline of cassis from Île d'Orléans layered with bitter chocolate brittle, served with a wild ginger sorbet and accompanied by a Premier Cuvée sparkling wine from Thirteenth Street Winery G.H. Funk Vineyards of Niagara. From first course to last, the 130 guests had experienced an explosion of flavours, colours, shapes, textures, and aromas. It was a meal that opened many eyes to the excellence and variety of Canadian food.

The same careful planning goes into every meal served at the nation's table, whether it's a breakfast for a handful of special visitors or a luncheon for a newly accredited ambassador or a state dinner. And sometimes the chefs come up with a dish that is truly inspired. One such success was the dessert served at the dinner for the recipients of the September 2003 Bravery Awards handed out at the Citadelle in Quebec City, the governor general's second official residence. The awards honour ordinary Canadians' extraordinary acts of courage, and the chefs climaxed the repast with a spectacular dish called Baked Athabaska, a reinvention of Baked Alaska. Baked Athabaska consisted of three different layers of ice cream—a maple and Manitoba red huckleberry sorbet, vanilla ice cream, and a bitter chocolate ice cream—surrounded by a flourless almond cake saturated with Le Sortilège, a maple syrup–flavoured whisky-based liqueur, which was served flambéed. If a single dish could reflect the energy and courage of the recipients of the Bravery Awards, this was it!

Cheeses to please any taste (*clockwise from top left*): Mi-Carême (Quebec); Violet Hill sheep cheese (Ontario); Blossoms Bleu (BC); Rideau Hall nut and berry bannock melbas (a great cheese accompaniment); Dragon's Breath Bleu (Nova Scotia); C'est Bon fresh goat cheese (Ontario); Mountain Meadow Brie (BC). Canada now boasts a remarkable number of raw milk or semi-pasteurized cheeses (cow, goat, and sheep), including a surprising assortment of blue cheeses. Quebec is the leader, but British Columbia is a strong second, with almost every other province now joining in.

Above: Crabapples from the Rideau Hall orchard. *Opposite*: Dwarf fruit trees in the Rideau Hall orchard are espaliered (trained so that their branches grow on a single plane) to save space and make the fruit easier to pick. The original orchard disappeared in the mid-twentieth century; the current orchard was planted in 2000 and includes several species of apple, plum, pear, and cherry. There are also new plantings of table grapes and wine grapes, as well as edible nuts.

The Rideau Hall Harvest

During the growing season, the chefs take full advantage of the organic herb and vegetable gardens on the grounds of Rideau Hall. Chef Bartsch visits the potager every morning during the growing season and often builds his menus around the produce that is ripe for harvesting that day. Lettuces and greens come early in the spring, as do asparagus, snow peas, and radishes. By midsummer the chefs are picking ripe heirloom tomatoes, several varieties of carrots, potatoes, beans, and zucchini, and an amazing range of fresh herbs. The gardens provide all types of vegetables—squash, cauliflower, and eggplant as well as a wide variety of Asian greens such as tatsoi, bok choy, and mizuna—well into November. And throughout the growing season the gardens and the property also yield an assortment of seasonal fruits and berries. From early spring until late October, the kitchen is almost completely self-sufficient in fruit and vegetables.

This garden bounty finds its way onto the plates served to guests at Rideau Hall in many different ways. Asian greens such as bok choy are sometimes mixed with coriander, fresh mint, and wild ginger or black mustard seed to create pungent aromas and complex flavours. The humble celeriac becomes a remoulade, a soup, a light purée, or a chip. Edible flowers such as chive blossoms, nasturtiums, and violas help dress up plates and appetizers. Some vegetables like squash or eggplant are grilled to bring out their full flavour. Miniature fennel is transformed into an anise salad.

In keeping with Rideau Hall's culinary philosophy, which is to respect what the earth offers and to use it in good time, the chefs are always thinking about what they can preserve so that some of the tastes of spring and summer are available in winter. Green tomatoes are made into chutneys, herbs create vinaigrettes, while basil and garlic become pesto sauce. Root vegetables are marinated and stored for the winter months. Homemade jams and jellies draw extensively on the garden harvest. And maple syrup from the Rideau Hall sugar bush finds its way into marinades, desserts, and sauces.

Canada, 1914
by
Plummer

Government House
Cook Book

Mail Orders promptly sent prepaid
upon receipt of Seventy-five Cents.
Address
Government House Cook Book
Dept. 2 — Post Office Box No. 234
OTTAWA : : : CANADA

MENU II

Minced Chicken Liver
and Mayonnaise Sandwiches
Sardine Paste Sandwiches
Duck Club Sandwiches
Cocoanut Sandwiches
Fresh Strawberry Jam Sandwiches
Lemon Wafer Cookies
Nut and Cream Layer Cake
Diamond Iced Cakes
Fresh Fruits
Iced Tea Iced Cocoa Iced Coffee
Bonbons

Strawberries with fresh grated cocoanut heaped over them and served with cream are delightful at five o'clock parties. Iced coffee and cocoa are delicious served with mock whipped cream. One cup of sugar, one large sour apple, and the white of one egg make about a pint. The apple is peeled and grated, and then all the ingredients are beaten together until the whole becomes a light froth; it is flavoured with vanilla. The apple must be mixed with the sugar as soon as it is grated to keep it from turning dark. There is no danger that the summer heat will turn this mock cream sour.

together and season to taste. Take 2 parts of cooked salad dressing and 1 part of oil mayonnaise. Mix together and add enough whipped cream to make it the proper consistence to pour. Add 2 potatoes and mix thoroughly together. Use enough of the dressing to make the potatoes quite wet.

POTATO SALAD. No. II.

1 quart cold boiled potatoes cut in small pieces, nearly the same amount of celery, 4 hard-boiled eggs, cut fine, and 3 medium-sized onions chopped fine; mix all together; season with salt and pepper; use oil mayonnaise; garnish with hard-boiled eggs and bleached celery tops.

N.B.—Diced cucumber may be used in place of celery and cooked dressing if preferred.

TOMATO SALAD GARNISHED WITH GREEN PEPPERS.

For each person to be served, choose a medium-sized tomato. Cut out the inside with a sharp knife and fill the tomato with cauliflower that has been simmering in salt and water until soft, and then chilled. Place the stuffed peppers on lettuce leaves and surround them with strips of green peppers arranged like the calyx of a flower. Serve with French dressing.

ARTICHOKE SALAD.

Another daintily pleasing salad from the South is prepared with hearts of artichokes—the canned ones serve very nicely for this purpose—pitted ripe olives, small bits of Neuchâtel cheese, and pecan nuts. Almost any green may be used to give the salad a pretty garnish.

SHRIMP SALAD.

Similar to a salmon salad is a salad of canned lake shrimp, boiled eggs cut into fine pieces, and chopped celery hearts. The ingredients should be mixed with a boiled egg dressing and should be served in a cored apple. When the apples have been filled, they should each be topped with a thin slice of tomato, a ring of green pepper covered with

Seating the guests is one of the most important problems to be dealt with in giving a dinner, especially if there are so many guests that general conversation is impossible . . . Crowding must be avoided, and to every four guests there should be one servant.

FROM THE GOVERNMENT HOUSE COOK BOOK

Pages from the *Government House Cook Book: Delectable Recipes and Hints to the Hostess* (1915), a local fundraiser that capitalized on Rideau Hall's reputation for fine dining. The book contains a grab-bag of North American and classic French recipes, which the editors promise "have behind them the traditions and experience of generations of good housekeepers." The recipes range from items like corned beef hash and candied sweet potatoes to fancier fare like cheese soufflé and steak Florentine and are interspersed with full-page advertisements for local Ottawa businesses such as Imperial Laundry and Hasting's Furs.

One recent event that beautifully illustrated the symbiosis between the kitchen and the garden was the Canada Day party held on July 1, 2003. Early that evening, about forty guests gathered on the upper terrace for some genuine culinary fireworks. For the first course, they dined on a lobster claw sitting on a minted basil salad of scallions, snap peas, and radishes served with a vinaigrette made of coriander and organic prairie colza oil. Next came Atlantic lobster tails marinated in a mixture of coconut milk, red curry, and tarragon, then skewered on lemongrass and grilled—a bold mixture of Eastern and Western perfumes.

The main course featured quail breasts marinated and seasoned with thyme and sage freshly picked from the herb garden, accompanied by a fricassee of garden broccoli, cauliflower, asparagus, and carrots. The final colourful touch for this dish was a layered ensemble of Swiss chard, spinach, and baby leeks folded in with shaved Roseval potatoes, served with a cream sauce.

An Eye for Tradition

The food served at Canada's House is, in many ways, on the cutting edge of contemporary Canadian cuisine, but the chefs also remain acutely conscious of historical roots and resonances. Sometimes the planning for a particular event requires extensive historical research. Such was the case for the spring 2003 opening of the exhibition "Culture and Democracy: Lord and Lady Elgin in Canada, 1847–1854," which highlighted some of the foundations of modern Canadian democracy. The 11th Earl of Elgin and Kincardine, the great-grandson of the governor general, came from his home in Scotland to attend the opening.

At the dinner given in his honour, Lord Elgin enjoyed a nineteenth-century feast with a few twenty-first-century flourishes: a Saskatchewan prairie chicken rappie pie from an old Acadian recipe that mixes meat with grated potatoes; fillet of northern Arctic char cured in Glen Breton whisky (the only single malt distilled in Canada); and grilled red-deer loin marinated in Singing Johnny, a cassis-based distilled liqueur popular in New Brunswick in the 1800s. The meat main dishes were served with a root vegetable and fayot (dried bean) fricassee.

Whatever the menu, the same basic principles guide the chefs at Rideau Hall: original dishes using fresh seasonal ingredients produced in an environmentally friendly way and showcasing Canada's bounty. This culinary laboratory never loses sight of its underlying purpose: to reflect Canadians to themselves and to the world.

Rideau Hall welcomes hundreds of foreign guests each year: heads of state and their entourages, ambassadors, industrialists and entrepreneurs, artists and thinkers. Each of them takes away a fresh impression of our country—and for many of them it is a radically revised idea of the world's largest northern nation. From the outside, Canada is still often perceived as primarily a wild land of vast uninhabited spaces, of moose and muskox and endless spruce forests, whose few inhabitants are either indistinguishable from Americans or ride around on horses wearing red coats and Stetson hats. Many of Rideau Hall's foreign guests are surprised to discover that Canadian wines are not only drinkable but excellent. Some are astonished to find that there is a "Canadian cuisine." They can't help but be impressed, not just because the meal is delicious but because the wines they drink and the foods they eat are also rooted in the place these products come from. They clearly celebrate their links to our northern land and its people: aboriginal, French, British, and multi-ethnic.

Oliver Bartsch puts the final touches on an unusual dessert comprising a beet-and-pumpkin-seed biscotto and a spiced apple–rosemary meringue tart.

There's another side to Rideau Hall's gastronomic diplomacy: promoting Canadian food and wine abroad. During the state visit to Iceland in 2003, for example, Canadian cuisine took centre stage at an event called "A Taste of Canada in Iceland," organized at the Reykjavik restaurant VOX. Under the guidance of Rideau Hall's executive chef, Oliver Bartsch, and executive sous-chef, Louis Charest, for three days Icelanders were able to taste foods from every region of Canada, paired with wines from Niagara and the Okanagan chosen by Pierre Laframboise.

VOX is one of the best restaurants in Iceland, renowned for its use of fresh, seasonal products. Before the event, the VOX

"It's Canadian!"

You get a wonderful sense of the whole country through the food served at Rideau Hall. The major official dinners are accompanied by rather long menus that describe the dishes in detail, where each ingredient comes from. It's also a way of supporting what Canadians are achieving right across the country. We really do have something to boast about—to each other and to the world.

At the December 2000 luncheon for the president of the Russian Federation and Mrs. Lyudmila Putina, President Putin—who is quite knowledgeable about food and wine—suddenly leaned over and said, "This wine is very good. What is it?" And we told him, "It's an Ontario Chardonnay." At first President Putin looked surprised. Then he turned to one of his officials and called out, "This wine's wonderful! It's Canadian!" *AC*

staff sampled the wines brought by the wine delegation of vintners from Ontario and British Columbia. They wanted to learn more about their unique characteristics so they could describe them to their patrons. They were also given a brief talk explaining why these specific wines would match well with the food being served during the event.

The invited guests for one dinner included the ambassadors of all the foreign countries posted in Iceland, as well as a number of Iceland's political and business leaders. During the meal, the guests sat with the Canadian vintners and had the opportunity to ask questions and share comments. They enjoyed bluefin tuna and Nova Scotia sea parsley tartare served on a Saskatchewan wild rice crisp, paired with a Riesling Family Reserve from Quails' Gate Winery in Kelowna, BC; Canadian Atlantic lobster foamy emulsion soup with tarragon oil, complemented by a Chardonnay from British Columbia's Mission Hill Family Estate; and grilled lamb chops with a golden squash purée, sage-flavoured lentil cake, baby green beans, and glazed shallots with eggplant ragout, paired with a Meritage Grand Reserve, a Bordeaux-type blend from the Okanagan Jackson-Triggs winery in British Columbia.

It was the first time that Canadian food and wine had been showcased on a state visit. The quality of both suprised the guests, most of whom were not aware that our country is a producer of fine New World wines. But Canadian gastronomic diplomacy is about more than signing commercial agreements and expanding export markets, important as these are. During a state visit, food can provide a common language for exchange and discovery between peoples. On state visits to Russia and Scandinavia, Canada's northern cuisine became part of an ongoing circumpolar conversation among countries that share the same latitudes and are dealing with many of the same issues: the rejuvenation of aboriginal cultures, the problem of overfishing, and the crisis of pollution in the High Arctic. That conversation is part of a much larger one that is taking place as Canada seeks to define its place in the twenty-first-century world.

Rideau Hall has always reflected Canadians to themselves and to others. It isn't surprising that its kitchens now mirror a very different country from the one Viscount Monck looked out upon from the newly renovated Rideau Hall in 1867. Over the years, the food served at Canada's House has evolved from traditional French cooking to a truly Canadian cuisine, just as Canada has progressed from being a country dominated by colonists from France and Great Britain into perhaps the most pluralistic society in the world. Canada is a young country, but no longer a shy one. It boasts an abundance of homegrown foods and wines from sea to sea to sea, and its cuisine celebrates the traditions of many peoples from many parts of the world. And these truths are evident to all who come to break bread at Rideau Hall.

Cut crystal set on the table of the Large Dining Room for a formal occasion.

Fiddlehead and Miramichi Bay Lobster Chowder with Fried Nova Scotia Sea Parsley

Grown in the gardens of Rideau Hall, fiddleheads are picked in early spring as soon as they sprout and before they open into ferns. Before using, fiddleheads should be boiled in water for four to five minutes to remove any toxins. Sea parsley, a form of dulse, is a type of seaweed farmed in Nova Scotia and New Brunswick and available only in dried form. It is a natural flavour enhancer; when fried, it tastes a lot like pancetta, an Italian-style bacon. In this chowder, the sea parsley acts as a garnish to add a distinct flavour and texture, similar to a crunchy crouton.

Suggested wine: Burrowing Owl Chardonnay

Serves 4

1 1/4 to 1 1/2 lb (560 g to 675 g) lobster
24 fresh fiddleheads
2 ounce (57 g) pancetta, chopped
2 tbsp (30 mL) extra-virgin olive oil
2 tbsp (30 mL) melted unsalted butter
1/2 cup (125 mL) diced onion
1/4 cup (62 mL) diced leek
1/4 cup (62 mL) diced carrot
1/4 cup (62 mL) diced fennel bulb
1/4 cup (62 mL) diced celery
2 tsp (10 mL) sea salt
2 tbsp (30 mL) all-purpose flour
4 cups (1 L) chicken stock
1/4 cup (62 mL) diced PEI potato
pinch each paprika and saffron
2 bay leaves
2 cups (500 mL) milk
1 tsp (5 mL) crushed peppercorns
1 tbsp (15 mL) chopped fresh tarragon or 1 tsp (5 mL) dried
1 tbsp (15 mL) chopped flat-leaf parsley or 1 tsp (5 mL) dried
1 clove garlic, minced
handful of deep-fried sea parsley (see sidebar on page 240)

Bring a large pot of water—no less than 1 quart (1 L)—to a rolling boil. Rinse the lobster under cold running water and quickly slide it into the pot. Bring the pot back to a rolling boil and cook the lobster for 3 minutes. Remove it and cool in an ice bath.

When cooled, place the lobster on a cutting board and split it from head to tail. Crack the claws and knuckles and remove the meat. Remove the meat from the tail too. Chop the lobster meat into bite-size pieces and place them in a covered container. Refrigerate them until ready to use.

Meanwhile, blanch the fiddleheads in a large pot of boiling salted water for 3 minutes. Remove them and quickly plunge in an ice bath for 30 seconds to stop the cooking

To fry sea parsley: heat 1/2 cup (125 mL) of oil in a small pot. When the oil is at 400°F (200°C), add the dried sea parsley. Once the sea parsley begins to pop, remove it with a slotted spoon, placing it on paper towels to absorb any excess oil.

process. Drain them, place in a covered container, and refrigerate until ready to use.

In a large stockpot over medium-high heat, cook the pancetta until it is just crisp and the fat is almost rendered, about 3 to 4 minutes. Add the oil, butter, onion, garlic, leek, carrot, fennel, and celery. Season the mixture with sea salt and cook for 3 minutes or until the onion is translucent. Add the flour and stir. Slowly add the chicken stock and continue stirring until the broth thickens. Add the potato, paprika, saffron, and bay leaves and continue simmering for 20 minutes. If not serving immediately, remove the pot from the heat and set aside.

When ready to serve, return the pot to the heat. Add the milk, peppercorns, tarragon, and parsley and gently bring the pot to a simmer. Remove the chopped lobster meat from the refrigerator, add it to the pot, and continue simmering for 30 seconds more. Serve immediately in warm soup bowls, garnished with fried sea parsley.

Butternut Squash Cannelloni Filled with Tarragon-Scented Polenta

The Rideau Hall chefs prepared this dish for a special luncheon for Queen Elizabeth II and the Duke of Edinburgh in October 2002. They reversed the original recipe by putting the vegetable on the outside—thin squash slices instead of pasta were used for the cannelloni—and the starch, in this case polenta, on the inside. The Parmesan hailed from Alberta—a Leoni-Grana cheese that is made in Camrose.

Suggested wine: Stoney Ridge Chardonnay Charlotte

Presentation
Serve the cannelloni generously drizzled with a good-quality extra-virgin olive oil or with a garlic-and-tarragon-infused olive oil. Either way you might add a few droplets of aged balsamic vinegar or a light tomato sauce.

Serves 4

- neck of one butternut squash, peeled and thinly sliced lengthwise into 8 slices
- 1⁄2 cup (125 mL) water
- 1⁄2 cup (125 mL) milk
- pinch salt
- 1⁄4 cup (62 mL) cornmeal
- 3 tbsp (45 mL) cold unsalted butter
- 1⁄4 cup (62 mL) freshly grated Parmesan
- 2 tbsp (30 mL) chopped fresh tarragon

Preheat the oven to 350°F (180°C). In a pot of boiling water, blanch the squash strips for 1⁄2 minute. Drain and plunge them briefly into cold water to stop the cooking process. Remove the strips and place them on a tray. (Blanching will make the strips pliable enough to be rolled without breaking.)

In a 2-quart (2 L) ovenproof saucepan, bring the water, milk, and salt to a boil. Slowly add the cornmeal while continuously whisking. As the mixture thickens, keep whisking to prevent lumps from forming. Once the mixture has thickened, cover the pot and place it in the oven for 25 minutes or until the grains are fluffy. Remove the polenta from the oven and stir in the butter, Parmesan, and tarragon. Allow it to cool at room temperature.

Using a pastry bag with a round tip 1⁄2 inch (1.25 cm) in diameter, pipe the polenta mixture across the bottom of each squash strip. Begin rolling the strips from the end with the filling. Once each strip is rolled into a cannelloni shape, trim the edges.

Cod Cake with Celeriac Ox-Eye Daisy Caper Remoulade

Celeriac is a gnarly, brown root vegetable (also known as celery root) that can be served raw or cooked. Either way, you'll need a knife—not a potato peeler—to remove its rough skin.

Contrary to popular belief, fresh Atlantic cod is still readily available at any fish store. But the ox-eye daisy caper might require a little more searching. Less salty and pungent in taste than a regular caper, it's made from the bud of the ox-eye daisy and can be found in some gourmet stores. If it proves to be too elusive, you can substitute regular capers.

Suggested wine: Gray Monk Estate Gewürztraminer

Serves 4

for remoulade

1/2 cup (125 mL) grated, peeled celeriac
1 tbsp (15 mL) chopped ox-eye daisy capers or regular capers
1/2 cup (125 mL) mayonnaise
1/4 cup (62 mL) sour cream
1 tbsp (15 mL) fresh lemon juice
2 tbsp (30 mL) chopped fresh dill
salt and pepper

for cod cakes

3 cups (750 mL) 2% milk
1 lb (454 g) cod
3 bay leaves
1 medium onion, diced
salt and pepper
12 ounces (340 g) PEI or Yukon Gold potatoes, peeled and cubed
1 large egg
1/2 cup (125 mL) fresh breadcrumbs
2 tbsp (30 mL) fresh lemon juice
5 scallions, finely chopped
5 drops Worcestershire sauce
pinch cayenne
pinch salt
3 tbsp (45 mL) olive oil

Presentation

Serve the cod cakes with the remoulade on the side. Garnish with a sprig of dill. A small salad of microgreens tossed with lemon juice and olive oil makes a great accompaniment for this dish.

for remoulade

In a medium bowl, mix together the celeriac, capers, mayonnaise, sour cream, lemon juice, dill, salt, and pepper. Set aside.

for cod cakes

In a large pot over medium heat, add the milk, cod, bay leaves, onion, salt, and pepper. Simmer, uncovered, for about 10 minutes or until the fish is just cooked. Remove from the heat and set aside to cool.

Meanwhile, in a separate pot, boil the potato in salted water for 15 to 20 minutes or until tender. Drain, place in a large bowl, and, while the potatoes are still hot, mash them thoroughly until they are smooth.

Remove the fish from the poaching liquid and crumble it into the mashed potato. Add the egg, breadcrumbs, lemon juice, scallions, Worcestershire sauce, cayenne, and salt. Mix well. Separate the mixture into four portions and form into cakes 3 1/2 inches (9 cm) around and 1 inch (2.5 cm) thick. Preheat a frying pan large enough to hold all four cakes; add the oil. Once the oil is hot, place the cod cakes in the pan and cook over medium heat for 2 minutes each side or until golden brown.

Zucchini Bread French Toast with Basil Sorbet and Nectarine Compote

Nothing could be simpler or easier to make than zucchini bread, which is also an excellent way to use up some of those excess zucchinis from your garden! In the hands of the chefs at Rideau Hall, zucchini truly becomes a celebration of summer's bounty. When making this delicious recipe, allow 24 hours to make the sorbet and the compote.

Suggested wine: Quails' Gate Optima Totally Botrytis Affected

Serves 4

for sorbet

1 1/2 (375 mL) cups water
3/4 cup (187 mL) sugar
1 tbsp (15 mL) corn syrup
1 cup (250 mL) coarsely chopped fresh basil, and 2 tbsp (30 mL) finely chopped
juice of 1 lemon

for compote

3 nectarines, peeled and diced
2 tsp (10 mL) melted unsalted butter
1/4 cup (62 mL) granulated sugar
1/2 tsp (2 mL) ground cinnamon
1/2 tsp (2 mL) ground nutmeg
1/2 tbsp (7 mL) grated fresh ginger or 1/2 tsp (2 mL) dried ginger
zest and juice of half a lemon
zest and juice of half an orange

for French toast

4 eggs (for zucchini bread)
3/4 cup (187 mL) granulated sugar
1/3 cup (83 mL) corn oil
1/3 cup (83 mL) fresh orange juice
1 tbsp (15 mL) orange zest
2 cups (500 mL) grated zucchini
1 2/3 cup (415 mL) all-purpose flour
3/4 tsp (4 mL) baking powder
3/4 tsp (4 mL) baking soda
pinch salt
1 1/2 tsp (7 mL) ground cinnamon
1/4 tsp (1 mL) ground cloves
2 eggs (for egg mixture)
3 tbsp (45 mL) 2% milk
butter for frying

Presentation
Garnish each slice with a scoop of sorbet and a spoonful of compote, and dust with a little icing sugar.

for sorbet
In a saucepan, bring the water, sugar, corn syrup, and coarsely chopped basil to a boil. Remove from the heat, add the lemon juice, and leave to infuse for 2 hours. Strain the mixture through a fine sieve and add the finely chopped basil. Place in a covered container and freeze overnight.

When ready to serve, take the sorbet out of the freezer. Using a stand mixer, preferably with a paddle attachment, beat the sorbet for 30 seconds or until it is softened. Return it to the freezer for a few minutes, then serve with the French toast and the compote.

for compote
In a sauté pan over medium-high heat, sauté the nectarines in butter and sugar for 2 minutes. Add the spices, juice, and zest; simmer for 2 minutes or until the nectarines are tender. Remove the compote from the heat, pour it into a bowl, cover it with plastic wrap, and refrigerate overnight.

for French toast
Preheat the oven to 350° F (180°C). With a stand mixer, beat the eggs and the sugar until the mixture thickens and forms ribbons; add the oil, orange juice, zest, and zucchini. In a separate bowl, mix and sift the flour, baking powder, baking soda, salt, cinnamon, and cloves. Add the sifted dry ingredients to the batter and continue mixing until they are just incorporated. (Be careful not to overmix.)

Butter and lightly flour a 4-inch by 10-inch loaf pan. Fill the pan with batter halfway up its sides. Place it in the oven and bake for 50 minutes or until a toothpick inserted in the middle comes out clean. Remove the pan from the oven and cool it on a wire rack for 10 minutes. Remove the loaf from the pan.

Before serving, slice the bread into ½-inch (1.25 cm) slices. In a bowl, add two eggs and milk and lightly beat. Dip the bread slices into the egg mixture so that both sides are fully coated; pan-sear them in butter over medium heat for 2 minutes on each side or until golden brown.

Île d'Orléans Crème de Cassis Mousseline and Bitter Chocolate Brittle

Crème de cassis fruit wine is made with black currants from the Île d'Orléans by a pioneer in the field, Bernard Monas. It is one of a number of Canadian fruit wines, mainly produced in Quebec, southern Ontario, and Nova Scotia, that are used in Rideau Hall desserts and sauces. This recipe is a slightly simplified version of one that appeared on the menu at the Order of Canada Awards Dinner in 2003. The mousseline was garnished with an elegant tuile and two sauces—crème anglaise and partridgeberry compote.

Suggested wine: Thirty Bench Special Select Late Harvest Riesling

Final preparation
Once the brittle has chilled, break it into 12 pieces of similar size (3 per plate). Place one brittle piece on each plate, spoon the mousseline onto the centre of the brittle, cover it with another piece, then alternate the mousseline and the brittle until each portion has three layers. Refrigerate until ready to serve.

Serves 4

for mousseline
3 1/2 sheets gelatin or 1 tbsp (15 mL) powdered gelatin
1/4 cup (62 mL) 2% milk
1/4 cup (62 mL) sugar
1 cup (250 mL) heavy cream
1/2 cup (125 mL) crème de cassis

for brittle
1 cup (250 mL) unsweetened chocolate
1 tbsp (15 mL) melted butter
1 cup (250 mL) finely chopped pecans and/or walnuts, divided into 2 portions

for mousseline
Soak gelatin sheets in cold water for at least 2 minutes, remove and squeeze out excess water by hand, and set them on a dish. If you are using gelatin powder, place it in a small bowl with 1/4 cup (62 mL) of cold water. Let it soak for at least 10 minutes and strain it.

In a saucepan on medium heat, stir the milk and sugar for 3 minutes or until sugar is dissolved and milk is heated through. Pour into a large bowl. Add the gelatin and allow to melt.

In another large bowl, whip the cream until soft peaks form. Slowly fold in the milk, sugar, and gelatin mixture. Add crème de cassis and, using a spatula, blend fully. Refrigerate for three hours until properly set.

for brittle
In a double boiler on medium heat, slowly melt the chocolate. Add the butter and stir until fully blended.

Add 1/2 cup (125 ml) pecans and/or walnuts. Remove from the heat and, using a spatula, spread the chocolate-nut mixture as thinly as possible on a parchment-lined tray.

Before the chocolate hardens, sprinkle on the remaining nuts. Place the tray in the refrigerator for at least 1 hour.

To contact Rideau Hall

By post	Rideau Hall 1 Sussex Drive Ottawa, Ontario K1A 0A1
By telephone	Toll-free anywhere in Canada and the United States: Main switchboard: 1-800-465-6890 Visitor services: 1-866-842-4422 In Ottawa: Main switchboard: (613) 993-8200 Visitor services: (613) 991-4422
By fax	(613) 998-1664
Email	info@gg.ca
Website	www.gg.ca

Hours for public tours of the Residence:

- Early May to late June: Saturdays and Sundays from 10 am to 4 pm
- Late June to early September: Daily from 9 am to 4 pm
- Early September to late October: Saturdays and Sundays from noon to 4 pm
- *The rest of the year by reservation only*

Tours are offered on statutory holidays from May to October.
Rideau Hall is a working residence and official events may require unforeseen changes to your visit.

Governors General (1867–Present)

1867-1868	Viscount Monck
1869-1872	Lord Lisgar
1872-1878	The Earl of Dufferin
1878-1883	Marquess of Lorne
1883-1888	The Marquess of Lansdowne
1888-1893	The Lord Stanley of Preston
1893-1898	The Earl of Aberdeen
1898-1904	The Earl of Minto
1904-1911	Earl Grey
1911-1916	Field Marshall H.R.H. The Duke of Connaught and Strathearn
1916-1921	The Duke of Devonshire
1921-1926	General The Lord Byng of Vimy
1926-1931	The Viscount Willingdon of Ratton
1931-1935	The Earl of Bessborough
1935-1940	The Lord Tweedsmuir of Elsfield
1940-1946	Major General The Earl of Athlone
1946-1952	Field Marshall The Viscount Alexander of Tunis
1952-1959	The Right Honourable Vincent Massey
1959-1967	Major General The Right Honourable Georges-P. Vanier
1967-1974	The Right Honourable Roland Michener
1974-1979	The Right Honourable Jules Léger
1979-1984	The Right Honourable Edward Schreyer
1984-1990	The Right Honourable Jeanne Sauvé
1990-1995	The Right Honourable Ramon John Hnatyshyn
1995-1999	The Right Honourable Roméo LeBlanc
1999-	The Right Honourable Adrienne Clarkson

Photography Sources

Preliminary pages
All photography by Nancy Tong except for the following: page iii: Rideau Hall—Bell Album—W. J. Topley; page vi: Rideau Hall; viii: Rideau Hall—A. J. Galpin Album—W. J. Topley; page ix: by Tony Beck; page x: Rideau Hall—A. J. Galpin Album—W. J. Topley; page xvii: National Archives of Canada (NAC) NAC/PA 9282 W. J. Topley

Part I
All photography by Nancy Tong except for the following: page 3: NAC/PA 8448 W. J. Topley; page 4: Rideau Hall—Maija Bismanis; page 5: NAC—F. J. Rubidge; page 6: Rideau Hall—W. J. Topley; page 7: NAC—C017540; page 12: NAC; page 15: NAC/PA 013180 W. J. Topley; NAC/PA 008485 W. J. Topley; page 18: NAC/PA 013180 W. J. Topley; Rideau Hall; page 20: Rideau Hall; pages 26 to 27, 48: by Lachlin McKinnon; page 29: Rideau Hall, attributed to W. J. Topley; pages 30 to 31: G. A. Pittaway/NAC; page 32: Rideau Hall—Bell Album—W. J. Topley; page 33: Rideau Hall—W. J. Topley; page 34: Rideau Hall—Bell Album—attributed to W. J. Topley; page 35: NAC/PA 8498 W. J. Topley; pages 36 to 37: Rideau Hall—Sir Shuldham Redfern, Secretary to the Governor General; page 39: Rideau Hall—A. J. Galpin Album—W. J. Topley; page 41: Rideau Hall—Bell Album—W. M. Notman & Son; Rideau Hall—Bell Album—Jules-Ernest Livernois; page 44: NAC/PAC 112693; page 45: NAC/PAC 168607 John Howe/NFB; page 54: Rideau Hall; page 57: Rideau Hall; page 58: Canadian Museum of Civilization; page 59: NAC

Part II
All photography by Tony Beck except for the following: pages 65, 66 (bottom), 113, 115, 118: by Sergeant Joanne Stoeckl; page 70: Rideau Hall—A. J. Galpin Album—W. J. Topley; page 74: Metropolitan Museum of Art; page 75: NAC/C 082887; page 78: NAC/C 082887; page 114: Rideau Hall—Bell Album; page 81: The Thomas Fisher Rare Book Library; page 88: Butchart Gardens Ltd., Victoria, B.C.; page 89: (left) Kingsbrae Garden, www.kingsbraegarden.com, Chris Flemming (right) courtesy of Metis Gardens; pages 94, 95, 103, 111, 116: by Lachlin McKinnon

Part III
All photography by Rob Fiocca except for the following: pages 150, 153, 161, 179, 225, 227, 234, 237: by Nancy Tong; page 154: courtesy of Saskatchewan Agriculture, Food and Rural Revitalization; page 156: reproduced with the permission of the Minister of Public Works and Government Services Canada, KGS-1073, by N. R. Gadd; page 157: (left) courtesy of the Government of Nunavut, (right) by Henry Ewert; page 158: Rideau Hall—A. J. Galpin Album—W. J. Topley; page 159: Rideau Hall—Bell Album; page 232: copyright, Canada, 1914 by L. E. Plummer; page 180: by Brian Atkinson; page 181, 186 to 187: by Lachlin McKinnon; page 183: Doug McLarty; page 184: Canadian Museum of Civilization, by Edward Sapir, no. 61251; pages 197, 199, 200, 202, 203, 205, 206, 208, 209, 210 to 211, 213, 214, 215: by Steven Elphick; pages 210, 211: by Tony Beck

Acknowledgements

So many people have contributed in so many different ways to my essay that it is hard to list them all, much less single any out. Having said that, I would like to express my gratitude to Melanie Kwong and the staff of the Rideau Hall archives and library for so patiently answering my queries; to Isabelle McLeod for her guided tour of Rideau Hall; to Barbara Uteck and Yves Chevrier for helping me to understand what life is like there; to Sara Angel and Louise Dennys and their teams at Otherwise Editions and Knopf Canada; and to Rosemary Shipton who did so much to make my text clear and readable.

—*Margaret MacMillan*

Thanks to Tony Beck who worked unbelievable hours to get these images, and the patience of Their Excellencies in walking the garden again and again to make us understand what they have done. Thanks to them for creating a garden of inspiration.

Special thanks to Ed Lawrence, Horticultural Specialist of the National Capital Commission, for his guidance and good sense; to Linda Dicaire, Senior Landscape Architect of the National Capital Commission.

And to the terrific gardeners of Rideau Hall: Roeland Jansen, Horticulturist Team Leader; Dagmar McCord, Heritage Garden Maintenance; Tim Welsh, Gardener; and Mark Burleton, Manager, Greenhouse & Grounds Services.

And Andréa Savoie, Executive Assistant to the Secretary to the Governor General, for organizing us all.

—*Marjorie Harris*

To my husband, Laurent Lavigne, my partner in crime and wonderful accomplice whose constant support and sound advice were essential to the writing of this part of the book.

To their Excellencies Adrienne Clarkson and John Ralston Saul, who have made me so proud to be Canadian.

To the people at Rideau Hall who worked countless hours helping me with this project, especially executive chef Oliver Bartsch, his sous-chef, Louis Charest, and their kitchen brigade; Pierre Laframboise, Jacques Gélineau, Christine MacIntyre, and her team.

To Tony Stewart, whose friendship, generosity and broad view of the Canadian wine industry were of invaluable help.

To Anthony Gismondi, for his sharp eye and useful suggestions.

To the vintners, winemakers, and chefs from Canada's two wine regions who shared their passion with me: Don and Elaine Triggs,

Len Pennachetti, Paul Speck, Jean-Pierre Colas, Tony De Luca, Linda Bramble, Dick and Ben Stewart, Judith Knight, Ingo Grady, Michael Allemeier, Senator Ross Fitzpatrick and his son Gordon, Tom Di Bello, Harry McWatters, Kenneth and Sandra Oldfield, and David Hawksworth and his wife, Annabel.

To all the chefs, growers, and artisan producers from across the country who made me appreciate our fascinating evolution towards a world-class distinctive Canadian cuisine.

To my editor-in-chief from *Le Soleil*, Yves Bellefleur, who was the inspiration behind this wonderful adventure.

To Rick Archbold, Sara Angel, and the people from Knopf Canada who believed in this project from the beginning.
—*Anne L. Desjardins*

Knopf Canada and Otherwise Editions offer thanks to Rick Archbold for his editorial oversight of this complex project, Rosemary Shipton and Gillian Watts for their skilled copy editing and proofreading, and Jonathan Howells and Fidel Peña at Dinnick & Howells for their direction on the book's design. Special thanks to the following at the National Capital Commission: Marcel Beaudry, Chairman; Michelle Comeau, Vice-President of Environment, Capital Lands and Parks; Christiane Bauer, Director of Official Residences; Ann Malone-Bianconi, Manager, Interior Design; to Paul LaBarge, President, and Harvey Slack, Executive Director, of the Canadiana Fund; and to the Advisory Council on the Official Residences of Canada. We are grateful for the support of the staff at Rideau Hall, including Patricia McRae, Research Officer; Christine MacIntyre, Director, Events Planning and Implementation; Curtis Barlow, Deputy Secretary, Policy, Program and Protocol; Executive Chef Oliver Bartsch; Executive Sous-Chef Louis Charest; Maurie Barrett, Librarian; Lachlin McKinnon, Special Advisor, and Keith Johnson, Volunteer. In particular we would like to thank Melanie Kwong, Program and Policy Officer, and Barbara Uteck, Secretary to the Governor General; without their involvement this project would not have been possible. Finally, we offer thanks to Her Excellency the Right Honourable Adrienne Clarkson, Governor General of Canada, and His Excellency John Ralston Saul for opening the doors of Rideau Hall and welcoming us at Canada's House.
—*Knopf Canada and Otherwise Editions*

A Note about the Type and Printing

Canada's House has been set in a digitized form of Bembo, a font family based on typefaces cut in 1495 by Francesco Griffo for an edition of Pietro Bembo's *De Aetna*. Griffo's original designs are regarded as among the first of the "old style" faces that were used as standard text types in Europe for 200 years. Bembo remains a preferred book face to this day because of its well-proportioned letterforms, functional serifs, and high readability. The italic is modelled on the handwriting of the Renaissance scribe Giovanni Tagliente.

Canada's House was printed at Friesens in Altona, Manitoba. The text stock is Luna Matte from Domtar Annacis Island in Delta, BC.